THE

5minute
DEBT SOLUTION

PRAISE FOR *THE 5-MINUTE DEBT SOLUTION*

"With Chris's coaching, I not only transformed my financial situation, but the program also significantly improved my marriage."

— Sharon Kasten, banker, Carlsbad, CA

"This program is a required ritual for anyone who wants to be wealthy."

— Tod Barnhart, author, *The 5 Rituals of Wealth* and *A Kick in the Assets*

"This type of program is a first for my wife and me and we love it! It created a dialogue between us that was long overdue. Finally, we are on the same financial page!"

— Mark Leon, schoolteacher, San Diego, CA

"People always say, 'I wish I knew then what I know now.' Well, as a young adult, I can certainly say I am glad I know this information now!"

— Dave Farrell, entertainer, Los Angeles, CA

"The Cookie Jar method is the missing link to your financial success! It is a simple strategy that anyone can do and it will make a huge difference in your long-term success!"

— Maria Olmos, ReMax Realtor, Long Beach, CA

"Chris is both informative and entertaining with a subject we often avoid dealing with. A fantastic program that I highly recommend."

— Steve Wright, network engineer, London, England

"Before we were married, my wife carried a lot of credit card debt, and consequently, a lot of negative beliefs about money. After following the guidelines in your course I saw a massive change in her, and as of now [January 1, 1999] we are completely out of debt! The best part by far is what this has done to our financial vision! Chris, keep reminding people how wonderful they will feel when they are in complete control of their financial future."

—Brian Rimor, entrepreneur, Denver, CO

"After using your CREDiT program, I eliminated more than $18,000 in credit cards in less than one year. This was an entire year earlier than my original plan. Thank you, Chris!"

— Jan Walker, advertising representative, New York, NY

"When it comes to finances, having a fundamental plan means every-thing! As a professional in the industry for 20-plus years, I have coun-seled many people and utilize numerous resources to help develop successful plans. Chris's ability to communicate and teach the compo-nents that are critical for success is refreshing and admirable. I recom-mend this book to any who are struggling to get started with or who have had a lapse in their plan to achieve financial independence."

— Kathryn W. Gerwig, CFP®, account executive, Corning, NY

"*There is a direct correlation to excess weight (fat) and debt. This book and the ideas set forth will help you lose this killer of your financial success.*"

— Jorge Cruise, *New York Times* best-selling author,
8 Minutes in the Morning and *The 3-Hour Diet*

"*I've read dozens of books on finance and didn't expect to be WOWED! Your writing style and the clarity of your message really made your book stand out and your inspiring words will get my year off to a great start.*"

— Martha C. Lawrence, author, *The Ashes of Aries*

"*The insights my husband and I received from this book have turned our finances around. We now have a plan we feel good about and we know financial independence is possible.*"

— Vivian Glyck, author, *The Tao of Poop* and
Founder of the Just Like My Child Foundation

ALSO BY THE AUTHOR

Products

For Take Count® "Live" Excel Workbook

This strategically designed Excel workbook does the thinking for you! With intuitive calculations for the exercises in The 5-Minute Debt Solution, this program will help you create the various game plans for your long-term success. Includes Create Your Savings Plan, Cookie Jars, New Spending Plan, Financial Independence goals, and many others. You can use these sheets over and over again to fit your changing circumstances and needs.

CREDiT Method™ "Live" Excel Workbook

This workbook takes you through a live version of Part One: Get Out of Debt Fast, helping you create your "massing of forces" strategy to get out of debt once and for all. All the calculations are done for you. Just fill out the questionnaire to see your strategy within seconds.

Destined for Wealth™ Workbook
112-page spiral bound version and downloadable PDF version available

Based on the 6 Master Steps for Financial Success, this detailed workbook outlines the steps for achieving financial independence. Complete with examples, exercises, and descriptions, it will guide you in establishing where you are financially, where you want to go, and how to create financial prosperity for yourself and your family.

Seminars, Speaking, and Individual Coaching

Destined For Wealth Webinar

This dynamic online program with Web support is available in groups (number of participants limited).

Destined for Wealth Full-Day Workshop (Public & Private Workshops)

This entertaining day outlines the steps for creating your financial blueprint and walks each participant through the process of creating a detailed, long-term plan for financial independence. Visit our website for scheduled events.

Destined for Wealth Keynotes

Chris is available for keynote speaking. Contact us for fees.

Destined for Wealth One-on-One Coaching

Work one-on-one with Chris as your coach for 6 appointments to create your individual plan.

For more information contact: **Eighty/Twenty Technologies, Inc.**
13024 Sandown Way, Suite 100, San Diego, CA 92130-3739
info@5MinuteDebtSolution.com or **www.5MinuteDebtSolution.com**

THE

5 minute
DEBT SOLUTION

Get Out Fast &
Stay Out Forever

CHRIS HENDRICKSON
FINANCIAL COACH

Foreword by Anthony Robbins
Author of *Unlimited Power* & *Awaken the Giant Within*

NEW YORK

THE 5-MINUTE DEBT SOLUTION

by Chris Hendrickson

Copyright © 2008 Chris P. Hendrickson

ISBN: 978-1-60037-430-2 Paperback

ISBN: 978-1-60037-431-9 Hardcover

Library of Congress Control Number: 2008923672

Published by:

Made Easy Publishing
An Imprint of
Morgan James Publishing, LLC
1225 Franklin Ave Ste 325
Garden City, NY 11530-1693
Toll Free 800-485-4943
www.MorganJamesPublishing.com

Cover Concept by:

Andy Wendt
Cromagnon Design
San Diego, CA

Cover Layout and Interior Design by:

Heather Kirk
www.GraphicsByHeather.com
Heather@GraphicsByHeather.com

DISCLAIMER

This book is designed to provide accurate and authoritative information on the subject of personal finances and borrowing. While all of the stories and anecdotes described in this book are based on true experiences, most of the names are pseudonyms and some of the situations have been changed slightly for educational purposes and to protect each individual's privacy. This book is sold with the understanding that neither the author nor the publisher is engaged in rendering legal, accounting, or other professional services by publishing this book. As each individual situation is unique, questions relevant to personal finances and specific to the individual should be addressed to an appropriate professional to ensure that the situation has been evaluated carefully and appropriately. The author and publisher specifically disclaim any liability, loss, or risk that is incurred as a consequence, directly or indirectly, of the use and application of any of the contents of this work.

DEDICATION

For my brilliant and beautiful wife Pamela, who always believed in me and knew I had the heart and talent to get this project onto paper. I will love you forever!

For my amazing "boyz" Jonathan and Benjamin. Your health, happiness, and impact on the world mean everything to me.

ACKNOWLEDGMENTS

It goes without saying that it takes a team to bring a project like this into fruition. I will be forever indebted to many people for their contributions, insights, support, and honest feedback.

First I'd like to thank my editor, the wonderful and talented Gail Fink, who took this project from good to outstanding. In addition, I'd like to thank my unofficial editor (and my mother-in-law), Carole Bigler, who helped me from day one. I can only hope that this project's impact parallels the difference you two made in its quality. I owe a special thanks to my very good friends Mike Koenigs, Vivian Glyck, and Jorge Cruise for constantly challenging me to keep plugging away and make this book a reality. I also appreciate the wisdom and insight given by Stephanie Abarbanel. Bob Simril, Lee Hendrickson, Ken Kinakin, Katherine Van Leeuwen, Lana Powers, Jared Rose, and Cliff Wilson reviewed early drafts of this manuscript; their contributions to improve the details of the book and the donations of their valuable time and feedback will not be forgotten. Also thanks to the very talented Andy Wendt at Cromagnon Design who made this project come to life with his brilliant design work. My gratitude goes to Marshonda Henderson for letting me share her inspiring story of financial turnaround and to all of my coaching clients who allowed me to learn with them, make the process more enjoyable, and make life better on a daily basis.

I would also like to acknowledge the ethical men and women who work in the lending industry. I respect your hard work and the care you take in trying to help people. Thanks to David Hancock and Joel Comm for believing in this project and offering to publish it through the Morgan James family.

Last, I would like to acknowledge my family—my two boys and especially my wife—who supported me every step of the way. Your love and pride in this work kept me up all those late nights and I am forever grateful for the sacrifices you made along the way.

CONTENTS

FOREWORD

Imagine yourself waking up tomorrow morning, well on the road to financial independence. You're finally in a position where you don't have to worry about money, and where you feel a true sense of freedom and security about your future.

You've got two to six months worth of income saved in secure investments to cover your expenses, just in case something happens. You're also putting a chunk of money into investments that grow more aggressively, such as stocks or mutual funds. Finally, you're saving toward your dreams—that new home or sailboat you've always wanted. You're also sharing your good fortune by contributing to others.

No matter who you are, what you do for a living, or where you currently are financially, you have the unlimited power right now to achieve your goals, realize your dreams, and become a force for good in your community or the world.

For more than three decades, my mission in life has been to help unleash that potential and ignite that spirit in everyone whose life I've had the privilege to touch. I've worked with 3.5 million people from 80 countries. I've had the honor of serving as an advisor to presidents, kings, and queens. I've coached some of the richest people in the world and people who are lucky if they make two dollars a day. By now, I'd have to

be crazy not to see that there are patterns in human experience. If you follow one set of patterns, you'll be angry, frustrated, and overwhelmed. Follow another and you'll likely be fulfilled, alive, and very rich—not just financially but in the ways that truly count: mentally, physically, spiritually, and in your relationships. I believe that what makes us the most fulfilled and truly wealthy is knowing that we're growing every day, which means we're striving to become more, give more, and never *settle for less than the lives we deserve.*

Eighty percent of success in life is psychology and 20 percent is mechanics. If you're not succeeding financially or in some other area of your life, you need to change your psychology. That means more than just how you think or feel. It's the power to learn and use what you learn, then take action on it. Once you've mastered the psychology, the mechanics will follow. It'll be easier to start achieving your financial goals and building a new future. When you start moving in the direction of your dreams, everything shifts.

I often say that *success leaves clues.* In most cases, many others have already succeeded in the same areas you want to succeed in, so you can learn from their most inspiring triumphs and most challenging mistakes. A good mentor or teacher can compress 20 years of hard-earned lessons into a few critical steps. The greatest gift you can receive is the ability to learn from another person's experiences, make them your own, and then succeed even more than that person did.

Chris Hendrickson offers an outstanding road map in *The 5-Minute Debt Solution.* He shares with you his innovative series of exercises and quick decision-making processes that helped him get out of debt for good and build a solid financial future for himself and his family. In *The 5-Minute Debt Solution,* you'll learn both the mechanics and the psychology of effective money management—how to build and maintain your money. Most important, you'll learn how to stay out of debt for good.

For my Wealth Mastery program, I invite some of the foremost financial experts in the world to share their practical and intuitive advice on how to build wealth and financial independence. However, you can't build wealth on a foundation of debt, and that's where Chris comes in. As a valued member of my team for more than 20 years, he has shared his powerful strategies for paying off debt fast with thousands of Wealth Mastery participants and many, many others.

Your decisions shape your destiny. If you're reading this book, you've probably decided it's time to live debt free. Chris will show you how. The true secret to mastering your finances or any area of your life is redirecting your focus and internalizing the methods that lead to deeper understanding so you can take the actions that make a difference.

Action is progress. You can start creating financial independence today by taking action: reading and applying the information in this book and tapping the richness that's already inside of you—your joy, your determination, and your gratitude for who and what you already have.

You've got everything you need within you right now to live the life of your dreams. My wish for you is that you wake up tomorrow refreshed and renewed, and with the help of *The 5-Minute Debt Solution,* be well on the road to financial independence.

Anthony Robbins
Chairman, Robbins Research International, Inc.
Author of *Unlimited Power* and *Awaken the Giant Within*

PART ONE

Get Out of Debt Fast

Every man is the architect of his own fortune.

~ Sallust

CHAPTER ONE
Living the American Dream—Or Are We?

Recently I attended a four-day conference focused on financial success. It was an extraordinary event that included some of the foremost experts in their respective fields—from world economy, investing, and trading to saving and taxes. As one of the experts, I was about to speak to nearly 800 people about getting out of debt and the psychology of financial success. Even though I had done this many times before, my heart was racing.

Just before I ran out on stage, I felt a sudden surge of overwhelming gratitude. It seemed like only a few short years had passed since the day when I was 26 years old and woke up, as I did on most mornings, totally stressed out about my credit card debt. On that particular day, I had to go to the bank, take out a cash advance on one of my credit cards, and deposit the money into my checking account to cover checks I had written to my creditors the day before. Talk about robbing Peter to pay Paul! Those checks were simply going to cover the minimum payments due to keep my debts from getting further behind.

Sick to my stomach, I entered the bank knowing that what I was about to do was completely against everything I believed about financial responsibility. How could I have created such a mess of my finances? What had gone wrong? Why had I allowed this to happen? I was frustrated and

deeply humiliated by the desperate situation I had created for myself. I didn't know what to do next or how to turn the situation around.

It was 1989 when I found myself in that horrible situation. In less than two years, I paid off my creditors entirely. I soon realized that I had the desire and knowledge to inspire others to do the same, and I've been doing just that ever since. As I heard myself being introduced at the conference, I bounded onstage. I was ready to rock the house!

Before we go any further, you should know that I am *not* an accountant, Certified Financial Planner, stockbroker, or professional money manager, nor am I a multibillionaire or mega business owner. I believe I am qualified to write and teach about financial solvency because I have been buried deep in debt and I got myself out. Since doing so, I have devoted my life to learning everything I could about debt elimination and I've shared my strategies and principles with thousands of people, helping them get out of debt, too.

What qualifies me to publish a book on this subject? This is an important question, because I strongly believe that you don't want to learn from just anybody. Although I don't know you personally, I suspect that you want to learn from people who have achieved positive results in their own lives and can teach you how to get the same or even better results. This strategy of learning from and improving upon other people's experience is called modeling, and modeling other people's success is the most productive and efficient way to re-create their success in your own life. Think about some of the greatest books ever written on personal and financial success. Books like the Bible, *Think and Grow Rich, The Richest Man in Babylon, The Success System That Never Fails, Unlimited Power,* and *The Millionaire Next Door* are all about modeling the successes of others. Through their stories and ideas, these books provide both examples of what to do and warnings of what not to do. In his runaway best seller *Rich Dad, Poor Dad,* Robert

Kiyosaki showed us what *to* do (lessons from his "rich dad") and what *not* to do (lessons from his "poor dad").

Let's face it. You don't want to ask someone who is obese how to lose weight or how to get healthy, and you certainly don't want to reinvent the wheel or learn by making your own painful mistakes if you can avoid them. Wouldn't you rather benefit from the experience of others, whether pleasurable or painful, positive or negative? Wouldn't you rather learn from a teacher or mentor who has not only accomplished something but who also knows how to teach it in a way that makes sense and motivates you to immediately use and apply the tools? A good teacher can move you to take action for your own reasons rather than anyone else's, including his or her own. I believe I fit this mold as a positive financial role model.

Years ago, I became obsessed with figuring out not only the strategies for getting out of debt but also for addressing the psychological aspects. It's not enough to get out of debt; you also have to *stay out of debt* so you can build the life you want and create independence for yourself and your family. This requires a shift in the way you think about and manage your money and finances. What good does it do to lose weight if you don't keep it off? Debt is the unwanted fat in your personal finances. It weighs you down; inhibits you from achieving your goals; and can eventually kill you physically, emotionally, spiritually, and financially. *The time to shed the excess weight of debt is now.*

I may not know you personally, but if you owe a lot of money to credit card companies or other creditors right now, I know what you're dealing with. I know how it feels when you're barely making ends meet and it seems as if you just get further and further behind. I know how you feel when creditors are calling your home so you don't want to answer the phone anymore. I also know how it feels when you're doing well financially in terms of income but you have so much debt that you never get to enjoy what you're earning. I've been there myself.

I've also been on the other side of the credit business. Early in my career, I spent years working for a major lending company that dealt exclusively in consumer loans. I saw firsthand what it was like for people to play this game without knowing the rules of financial success and what that could do to their spirit. I stood in court and saw the look in people's eyes as they lost their property and could do nothing about it because they lacked the resources to turn things around.

I left the consumer finance industry out of total disgust for what was being sold: money at a high cost to people who couldn't afford to borrow any more. I remember the pained look in people's eyes as they helplessly watched me take their property and could do nothing about it. They thought they were living the American dream, when in fact they had borrowed against it at an exorbitant interest rate. My goal and desire for you is to give you the resources and strategies to master this part of your personal finances once and for all.

WHERE ARE YOU HEADING?

In my opinion, financial independence is one of the most important goals we can achieve. It is our birthright to pursue happiness, personal financial independence, and economic security for our families and ourselves. We deserve it. Many of us, however, have developed all kinds of obstacles that get in the way of achieving true financial success. These obstacles come in many forms: beliefs; religious ideas; fears and feelings of inadequacy and low self-esteem; impulsive and compulsive spending and other negative financial patterns, habits, and behaviors; confused values and rules; a lack of clarity about our personal financial vision; and conflicting goals.

There's a difference between seeking to amass a lot of money and material possessions and building lasting wealth and financial prosperity. People can get confused about what they are ultimately after by focusing on the size of their bank accounts and the amount of "stuff" they have. Think about it. Did any of us grow up saying to ourselves, When I get older, I want to owe a lot of money to multiple lending institutions so I can work my butt off trying to keep up, just to fund their revenues and profits? I don't think so. However, this is what's happening. Lending institutions get bigger and bigger while most consumers get further and further behind.

As I write this in 2008, outstanding debt in America has skyrocketed to its highest level in our nation's history and, like obesity, borrowing for consumerism has become epidemic. As consumers we owe nearly $2.5 trillion (not including mortgage debt) and as individuals we owe more than $9,659 on our credit cards at an average interest rate of 14.67%, according to current Federal Reserve Board statistics. The average household has more than 10 credit cards, and 500 million new cards are issued every year in North America, according to Cardweb.com, a leading online publisher of payment information. At nearly 14%, our debt service burden (the ratio of our debt payments to our disposable income) is close to the all-time high.

We're also not saving. In 2005 and 2006, our personal savings rate dipped into the negative and was on track for a third straight negative year, according to the U.S. Commerce Department. In 2006 the rate was *minus* 1%, the lowest since 1933, which was considered the bottom of the Great Depression.

According to statistics compiled by the Administrative Office of the U.S. Courts and Cardweb.com, bankruptcies have skyrocketed again, even after new laws in October 2005 made filing more difficult. In 2005, a record 2 million people filed for bankruptcy. In 2006, the first full year under the new laws, filings dropped significantly to 617,660. However, comparing the first three quarters of 2006 to the first three quarters of 2007, filings increased more than 40% and filings in the third quarter of 2007 were 84% higher than they were in the first quarter under the new laws (218,909 in Q3-2007 compared to 116,771 in Q1-2006). There is a

direct correlation between overspending (which ultimately leads to borrowing) and filing for bankruptcy protection. Later I will show you how every dollar you pay in interest adds up to *double* that amount subtracted from your dreams and goals.

As a nation we are spending more than we earn and saving nothing. That is the exact opposite of the number one key for financial success, which is to spend less than you earn and invest the difference. *Unless you take the right steps today, you may have little chance of retiring or achieving any type of quality lifestyle without continuing to work for it.* And since we're living much longer than earlier generations, our extra years will have to be paid for somehow. Wouldn't you rather have the decision to keep working be a choice instead of a necessity for keeping your head above water?

WHAT IS *THE 5-MINUTE DEBT SOLUTION*?

The 5-Minute Debt Solution is a simple five-step process for creating a compelling plan to get out of debt once and for all. The key word here is *compelling.* In studying and teaching this material since the early 1990s, I have found that if people don't have a compelling plan, they will not follow through—period! My commitment to you is to compel you to create the plan and then have you follow through on it until you are debt free. I will also show you how to *stay* debt free and start on the path to financial independence. *What* to do is simple; *how* to do it is simple, too. The difference with this system is *why* to do it.

In the title of this book I've promised a five-minute solution and I want to explain what that means. First, let me tell you what it doesn't mean. This book is not about getting rich quick, since I believe that game plan rarely works. Furthermore, if you think you'll be out of debt within the first five minutes of picking up this book or five minutes after reading it, you're seeking a result I cannot deliver. I'm not a magician; like you,

I live in the real world. It may take you a little time to digest the material and implement it.

So, what is the five-minute solution? It's a series of exercises and decision-making points that will take no more than five minutes each. In fact, some of the exercises and decisions will take only a *moment!* In that moment you make a choice that cuts off every other possibility and you begin to build new momentum toward your financial goals and dreams. I can tell you this with total certainty because I have worked with people one-on-one, in small groups, and in larger groups of nearly a thousand. People often tell me, "I met you last year, used your program, and now I'm totally debt free." The solution to their debt problem was inevitably the result of a *decision* they made one year earlier, in a moment, simply by answering a few questions.

ANSWERED QUESTIONS ARE THE KEY

We'll be working together to answer questions that will solve your credit, debt, and financial problems. The Bible says, "Ask and you shall receive," but asking is only the first step. You can't just ask; you must *answer* the question. Answer *honestly* and *specifically* and you will *receive even more.* Take a moment to think about a decision you made recently to improve your life. Maybe you decided to stop smoking, start exercising, get married (or divorced), get a raise or promotion, or change careers. If you think about it, you can probably trace the decision back to a specific moment when you said, "This is it, I've decided," or "Starting right now I choose A over B, this over that." You had powerful emotion behind the decision and your reasons were stronger than any obstacle that stood in your way. Whether you realize it or not, you made the decision because you either consciously or unconsciously started asking yourself new or better questions.

In this book, I will help you create the motivation to complete the exercises, make critical decisions, and back them up with your own

reasons. I will also help you generate the emotion to make well-thought-out and powerful choices instead of choices made in a pumped-up moment that you'll give up after a short time or as soon as you hit the first obstacle. *The 5-Minute Debt Solution* is a simple and powerful approach. It may not always be easy, but I think you'll find the process rewarding as you start your journey toward your own debt freedom and financial independence.

The 5-Minute Debt Solution is also a workbook, or as I like to refer to it, a playbook. When you watch a football game, you always see the coach on the sideline with a book or laminated card in his hands. This is the team's playbook, designed to assure their victory as they carry out their game plan to a winning outcome. Money, finances, debt, and credit are just that: a game you can win once you know your plan and abide by the rules you've set for yourself. This book was designed to help you determine exactly what you want and need to accomplish in each of the critical areas to assure your success. It also includes accelerators—ideas, strategies, and exercises you can implement to get the results even faster.

In the following pages, you'll learn about the most important elements that determine whether or not you'll achieve financial independence. You'll learn strategies that will equip you with the psychology to assure your success in this important area of your life. You'll also learn how to determine precisely where you are right now by counting all you have, all you spend, all you owe, and all you earn. You'll evaluate how you're doing by using an accurate model for determining whether you're winning the game or not.

Using a process I call the CREDiT Method™, you'll answer five critical questions that begin with a decision and lead to immediate, result-producing actions. I'll help you discover or refine your financial purpose or mission, understand the three types of financial goals, and learn how to set what I call critical goals. You'll create your "company" for financial success and learn to watch what you say and how to change the beliefs that hold you back. You'll learn how to calculate your net worth and, most important, you'll learn how to get out of debt fast and stay out of debt forever. I'll show you how to measure and monitor your goals and acquire resources for continued success. Finally, this book will help you understand the consequences of your financial decisions, no matter how small they may seem.

You may not feel that you have a lot of debt, but if you have *any* debt at all, you'll find value in reading and using this book. If you feel you need help staying out of debt and creating a plan to build financial independence, you'll gain momentum by reading this material. If you owe a lot in credit card debt, you'll save thousands of dollars, if not tens of thousands and possibly even hundreds of thousands, by using the ideas and strategies in the following chapters. Financial independence is within your grasp. It is noble, you deserve it, and you can achieve it.

I hope I have provoked and intrigued you enough to read on. If you get nothing else from this book but the inspiration to make improvements in your financial world, no matter how small, then I will consider it a win because I have learned that *even the smallest decision can have a huge positive impact on your life.* Unfortunately, the same is true on the negative end as well: not deciding to do something, no matter how small it may seem, can create financial ruin and despair.

KNOWLEDGE + ACTION = POWER

Before we go any further, I'd like to acknowledge you for reading this book. You're obviously eager to improve your financial situation, and you want more for yourself and your family. I know there are hundreds of other books competing for your time and attention, and I

respect you for choosing this book. I truly hope you're committed to reading it and using the material.

If you simply read this book, you may get some good ideas and you may even become motivated. However, you will get lasting value only if you put the plan to work for you. Motivation by itself is not enough. You must also take action to see the results. It's like joining a gym or athletic club to improve your body. It's not enough to buy a membership; you have to go work out. You have to exercise, and that's what I've created for you in this book.

There are dozens of books on the market about how to get out of debt. I've read almost every one of these books for you. A few are excellent, some are good, but most are poor because they lack strategy, psychology, and exercises. I often become frustrated when I read a chapter that has some good ideas but doesn't ask the reader to do anything. I believe you have to do something in the moment or you'll lose the power of what you've just read.

You don't need another book with a lot of text in it. I believe people crave a powerful mind-set and a simple, strategic game plan for accomplishing their goals. That's what the five-minute process is about. Rather than boring you with superfluous language, this book gives you critical ideas and principles, in as brief a time frame as possible, and then gives you strategies and exercises to help you put the principles to use.

To get measurable results, you have to combine knowledge with action. To be successful, you must also blend your knowledge and action with the ability to recognize whether your actions are getting you closer to your goal. If they aren't, then you have to do something different until you get what you're after. This truism applies to every area of your life, not just finances.

In this chapter we have begun our journey. I am honored and privileged to be your coach as we work together to create your path to freedom from the burden of debt and build your financial independence. In the next chapter we'll start the process by taking stock of your current financial situation. Let's get started.

Whatever you vividly imagine, ardently desire, sincerely believe, and enthusiastically act upon must inevitably come to pass.

~ Paul Meyer

CHAPTER TWO

Wealth Navigation: Taking Count of Your Finances

It seems like everyone has the secret formula for success. Stephen Covey wrote about the seven habits, Suze Orman promised us nine steps, Tod Barnhart wrote about five rituals, and Robert Allen and Mark Victor Hansen promoted the idea that we could be millionaires in one minute. Even as far back as 1926, George Clason wrote about the "seven cures for a lean purse" in his book *The Richest Man in Babylon* (which happens to be one of my personal favorites and a book I highly recommend). So, which is it: five, seven, nine, one, two, or three?

The truth is, it's none of the above and it's all of the above. The right answer is whatever serves you in the moment and helps you focus on what you need to focus on, change what you need to change, and get moving in the direction you need to move. All of the preceding authors have helped me personally in many ways and they have helped millions of others as well.

If you want an honest assessment, there are probably 4 million actions to financial independence. If I were to look back at *all* the steps or actions I've taken to get where I am today, I would be able to count at least several thousand of them. I realize this sounds like a contradiction since I talked about five steps in the introduction, but are you really going to pick up a book called *The 4 Million Steps to Financial Independence*?

Of course not! You'd get tired just reading the title, much less trying to carry out the plan. As authors, teachers, or mentors who provide debt solutions, we take these 4 million steps and condense them to what we believe are the most critical in getting people to move in a better direction. Peak-performance coach Tony Robbins, a friend and significant mentor in my life, calls this skill chunking.

Chunking is a critical technique in the learning process when you're faced with too much information or too many ideas to absorb all at once. Think about trying to remember a phone number. You will more than likely have trouble if you try to remember it as 10 numbers all in a row or as one cluster of numbers. But when you chunk it into three parts (area code, prefix, and the remaining four digits), you are better able to remember it and sometimes unable to forget it. The same is true for a social security number. Have you ever noticed it is written out as 123-45-6789 (chunks of three, then two, then four)? Pull out your Visa or Master-Card and notice that the account number is broken into four chunks of four numbers (although it's probably not a good idea to memorize this one). Our brains tend to remember things best when they are grouped into sets of three. Keeping ideas to two, three, or no more than four is best for the learning (and remembering) process.

This book is about how to chunk your financial life in regard to getting out of debt as fast as possible, staying out forever, and building your financial independence. These three chunks are easy to understand and simple to follow. Anyone can accomplish them. As important as it is to win the credit and debt game, that's just one piece of the financial pie. In the next few pages I take you through a brief but powerful process I call Take Count®. This procedure is meant to get you thinking about your finances as a whole (a bigger chunk, if you will) and set you up for *total financial success* rather than dealing with only the critical step of getting out of debt. If we lay this foundation together and get really clear on where you are, you'll be much more likely to follow through on your get-out-of-debt plan, which is my ultimate desire for you. Then, after you count all your finances, I'll take you through my Money Metrics™ process so you can evaluate how you're doing by using some basic and reasonable measuring sticks (metrics) for success.

To use our health analogy again, I believe that people who lose weight and keep it off do so because they make an honest assessment of their current health and they create a clear vision of what they want in the future. They also build a foundation based on mental and emotional health, so that when they start executing their plan, they are poised for longer lasting success than someone who simply goes on a diet.

If you merely read or scan these pages without following through with the exercises, you may become enlightened and you may even become inspired. On the other hand, if you follow along and fill out the forms on these pages honestly and accurately, you will empower yourself financially and create a whole new financial destiny for yourself and your family. If you like, you can download an automated Excel spreadsheet of this entire process that will calculate your evaluation scores for you. Please go to www.5MinuteDebtSolution.com for a copy.

THE TAKE COUNT PROCESS

If you wanted to go to a desired destination, which way would you go? Would you go north, south, east, west, or a combination thereof? Of course it depends on where you are to start with. *You can't figure out how to get where you want to go until you know where you currently are.* In the financial game, I call the process of figuring out where you are Take Count.

Step 1: Count Your Current Assets

The first thing to count is your current assets. Using tables 2.1, 2.2, and 2.3, you will capture your *account* assets (liquid and illiquid savings and investment accounts) and your *personal* and *household* assets (the items of value you own). Before you begin, please be sure to gather the necessary information and a calculator. You'll need:

- Bank account statements
- Portfolio or brokerage statements
- Insurance or annuity policies and/or statements
- Retirement account information, such as 401(k), IRA, etc.
- Real estate appraisal documents
- Documents or ledgers that list household and personal assets

Since accomplishing your financial goals is really a journey, I am using the analogy of mapping out a journey, and in any journey you have to navigate. I would like to be your copilot as we travel together. This is where your real journey begins, so please don't just look at these tables: take the time right now to fill them out to the best of your ability and then we will move on to the next component.

TABLE 2.1 INVESTMENT ASSETS (LIQUID)

Annuities (surrender benefit of any annuities you own):	$
Bonds (value of corporate, municipal, or global bonds):	$
CDs (amounts you have in certificates of deposit):	$
Commodities (value of any commodities or futures you own):	$
Pension Fund/SEP (value of these or similar types of accounts):	$
Investment Real Estate (fair market value of any buildings or properties you own):	$
IRA Accounts (amounts in traditional or Roth IRAs):	$
Life Insurance (cash or redemption value of policies you own; do not include death benefit):	$
Money Market (any amounts you have in money market accounts):	$
Portfolio Accounts (amounts you have in stocks and/or mutual funds):	$
Savings Accounts (amounts you have in regular savings):	$
401(k) Accounts (any amounts you have in retirement funds):	$
403(b) or Keogh Accounts (any amounts in these or similar accounts):	$
Subtotal Liquid Investment Assets:	$

TABLE 2.2 INVESTMENT ASSETS (ILLIQUID OR PLANNED SPENDING)

Business Partnerships (value of any business interests you have):	$
Checking Accounts* (amounts you have in any regular checking accounts):	$
Education/College Savings (value of any 529 or similar plan):	$
Real Estate (value of your current residence only):	$
Any Other Illiquid Investments (any money you have in an account):	$
Subtotal Illiquid or Planned Spending:	$

*The balance of your checking account is listed under planned spending, assuming that you may be spending this money on an upcoming or anticipated expense.

TABLE 2.3 PERSONAL/HOUSEHOLD ASSETS

Automobiles (any autos or vehicles you own):	$
Art and Collectables (paintings, heirlooms, coins, etc.):	$
Electronics (computers, stereo equipment, phones, games, handhelds, etc.):	$
Household Items (furnishings, appliances, etc.):	$
Jewelry (include all items of significant value):	$
Luxury Items (yacht, plane, etc):	$
Toys (boats, motorcycles, jet skis, etc.):	$
Any Additional Assets (any other assets you own of significant value):	$
Subtotal Personal/Household Assets:	$
Total All Assets (Liquid, Illiquid, and Personal/Household):	$

Great job! Please make sure you have filled in the totals since you will carry them over to the evaluation pages shortly.

Step 2: Count Your Debts and Liabilities

Next you take count of your debts and liabilities. Here you will capture all monies you owe. Before you begin, please be sure to gather the necessary information, including:

- Mortgage statements
- Loan documents
- Credit card statements
- Medical bills
- Collection accounts
- Any additional debt records or statements

You'll work with this piece in much greater detail in chapter 5 of this book to create your plan for total debt elimination.

TABLE 2.4 DEBTS AND LIABILITIES

Type of Debt/Liability	Total Balance Owed	Minimum Mo. Payment
Automobile Loan(s) (amounts you owe on your vehicles):	$	$
Business Loans (amounts you owe on business):	$	$
Credit Cards (include banks, department stores, gas cards, etc.):	$	$
Education Loans (amounts you owe for college, trade school, private school, etc):	$	$
Personal Loans (consumer credit loans, family members, friends, loan sharks, etc.):	$	$
Mortgage(s)* (list principle & interest for your current residence only):	$	$
Mortgages: Rental/Vacation Property (any mortgages on investment property):	$	$
Retail Installments (include revolving credit purchases):	$	$
Any Additional Debt (back taxes, medical bills, collection, liens):	$	$
Total All Debts:	$	$

*Be sure to exclude your property taxes and/or any insurance that may be included in your monthly mortgage payment.

Keep in mind that I did not ask you to list any debts for which you may have cosigned, but it is critical to mention that this is your debt, too, should the primary borrower default on the loan.

Step 3: Count Your Monthly Income and Taxes

Taking count of your monthly income is the next essential step for financial planning. Before you begin, please gather the necessary information (such as pay stubs, tax returns, etc.) that will help you complete the questionnaire as quickly and accurately as possible. If your income fluctuates from month to month or year to year (such as occurs with sales commissions or contract work), simply use your *average* over the past 6 to 12 months.

You can gather information about your monthly tax obligations from your paycheck, whether you receive one monthly, weekly, or every other week. If you are a 1099 contractor, you will need to refer to your previous year's taxes. Simply take your prior year's gross annual income and divide it by 12 to determine the monthly total.

TABLE 2.5 MONTHLY INCOME AND TAXES

Your Monthly Income (wages, salary, commissions):	$
Spouse or Partner's Income (wages, salary, commissions):	$
Bonus Income (performance, quarterly, yearly, holidays, etc.):	$
Other Family Income:	$
Dividend or Interest Income:	$
Pension or Trust Income:	$
Any Additional Income (business interests, rental properties):	$
Toys (boats, motorcycles, jet skis, etc.):	$
Gross Monthly Income:	$
Less All Taxes (include federal, state, social security, Medicare, disability/unemployment insurance):	$
Net Income (aka Take-Home Pay) (total All Income less All Taxes):	$

Step 4: Count Your Monthly Expenses

Taking count of your monthly expenses is the next step in creating your financial plan. Again, before you begin, please be sure to gather the necessary information that will help you fill out the questionnaire to the best of your ability (and again, as accurately and honestly as possible), including:

- Checking account registers
- Credit card statements
- Receipts
- Paycheck stubs
- Tax documents

Failing to capture all of your information could throw you off course. You may have expenses not listed here; therefore, you need to stop and think carefully so your list of expenses is as accurate and complete as possible.

TABLE 2.6 MY SEVEN CRITICAL MONTHLY EXPENSES

1. Rent or Property Taxes (if you own, list property taxes only):	$
2. Food–Groceries only (include food and household groceries):	$
3. Clothing/Grooming (include basic clothing, haircuts, makeup):	$
4. Auto/Transportation (service, fuel, parking, registration):	$
5. Insurances (life, disability, medical, HMO, auto, PMI, legal, home/hazard):	$
6. Utilities (gas/electric, cable, phone, cell phone, water, trash, sewer):	$
7. Total Minimum Monthly Payments (from the Debts and Liabilities worksheet, table 2.4):	$
Total Seven Critical Expenses:	$

TABLE 2.7 MY DISCRETIONARY MONTHLY EXPENSES

Business Expenses (any un-reimbursed business expenses):	$
Child Expenses (day care, nanny, babysitter, child care or support, camp):	$
Clubs/Organizations (dues for gym, athletic club, magazines, environmental, community, etc):	$
Contribution (political, charity, church, tithing, donations):	$
Education (college, continuing education, personal growth seminars, books/CDs):	$
Electronics/Technology (computers, audiovisual, PDA, cell phones, pagers, MP3 players, etc.):	$
Food/Dining Out (restaurants, snacks, coffee, vending machines):	$
Financial/Banking (broker fees, annual fees, service fees, ATM, etc.):	$
Fun/Entertainment (concerts, shows, movies, clubs, video rental, CDs):	$
Gifts (birthdays, anniversaries, holidays, weddings, babies, etc.):	$
Habits (cigarettes/tobacco, alcohol, gambling, etc.):	$
Hobbies/Activities (sporting, camping, golf, scuba, skiing, painting, etc.):	$
Household Groceries (toiletries, paper goods, cleansers, laundry, etc.):	$
Household Items (furniture, appliances, decorative items, kitchen/bath):	$

Household Maintenance (windows, carpets, paint, etc.):	$
Household Staff/Support (security service, maid, gardener, pool, etc.):	$
Legal/Professional Fees (attorneys, CPAs, financial advisors, etc.):	$
Luxury Items (yacht/boat, airplane, limousine, spa retreats, etc.):	$
Medical/Dental/Alternative (glasses, prescriptions, massage, chiropractor, acupuncture, herbs/supplements, etc.):	$
Personal Accessories (jewelry, purses, hats, sunglasses, etc.):	$
Pet Care (veterinarian, food, toys, supplies, etc.):	$
Rentals/Properties (mortgage payment and all expenses, upkeep, etc.):	$
Toys (motorcycles, boats, jet skis, etc.):	$
Travel/Vacations (airfare, hotels, timeshares, car rental, activities, etc.):	$
Any Other Expenses:	$
Subtotal Discretionary Expenses:	$
Total All Monthly Expenses (Seven Critical Expenses plus Discretionary Expenses):	$

Money Metrics: Are You Winning or Losing the Game?

After you have completed the Take Count process, you must evaluate how you are doing. Are you winning the game? Breaking even? Or are you losing the game? One of the great things about personal finances is that if you want to know how you're doing, you simply need to count. Then compare what you have to what you ultimately want and when you want it so you can gauge how you're doing in relationship to the two. Take a few moments right now to complete the following exercises so you can find out how you're doing. A calculator will be helpful in this process and then I'll see you on the other side.

TABLE 2.8 INCOME/EXPENSES

Income/Expenses		My Score
Total All Monthly Income (total from table 2.5)	$	
My Seven Critical Expenses (total from table 2.6)	$	**Evaluation Scale** 0–40% = A 41–50% = B
Percentage (divide your Seven Critical Expenses by your Gross Monthly Income)	%	51–60% = C 61–70% = D 71% & above = F

TABLE 2.9 DEBT TO INCOME RATIO

Debt to Income Ratio (aka Debt Service Burden)		My Score
My Minimum Debt Payments (total from table 2.4)	$	
My Monthly Income (total from table 2.5)	$	**Evaluation Scale** 0–10% = A 11–20% = B
Debt Payment Ratio (DPR) (divide Total Minimum Monthly Debt Payments by your Gross Monthly Income)	%	21–30% = C 31–40% = D 41% & above = F

TABLE 2.10 ASSETS/LIABILITIES

Assets/Liabilities		My Score
Total All Assets (total from table 2.3)	$	This is a subjective figure and can only be graded based on a few criteria. Rather than evaluating this figure, you will evaluate your *Critical Mass* in table 2.12
Total All Debts (total from table 2.4)	$	
My Net Worth (subtract All Debts from All Assets)	$	

TABLE 2.11 DAILY OPERATING INCOME VS. EXPENSE

Daily Operating Income vs. Expense		My Score
My Daily Income (divide Total Monthly Income from Table 2.5 by 30)	$	
My Daily Expense (divide Total Monthly Expenses from Table 2.7 by 30)	$	**Evaluation Scale** 0–70% = A 71–80% = B 81–90% = C 91–99% = D 100% & above = F
Daily Income to Expense Ratio (divide Daily Expenses by Daily Income)	%	

HAVE YOU SAVED 10%?

In *The Richest Man in Babylon*, George Clason explains that the number one key to financial success is to *spend less than you earn,* and he specifically defines that standard as saving a minimum of 10% of your gross earnings. If we are to use this as our measuring guide, my question to you is *have you been doing this*? Let's do one more exercise in the evaluation process to check on this important principle and find out whether you need to make a shift in this area.

1. **Determine your total lifetime earnings to date.** There are two ways to do this. Either multiply your annual average income by the number of years you have worked, or contact the Social Security Administration at (800) 772-1213 to request a Social Security Statement form, which will show all of your recorded earnings over your lifetime (you can also download the form from www.ssa.gov/online/ssa-7004.pdf).

    Lifetime earnings to date: $_____

2. **How much money in the form of cash and investments do you currently have?**

    (Liquid investments from table 2.1) $_____

3. **What percentage does this represent?**

    (Divide #2 by #1) _____%

4. **How did you score?**

TABLE 2.12 MY SAVINGS SCORE

My Score
Evaluation Scale 10% & above = A 7–9% = B 4–6% = C 1–3% = D Less than 1% = F

It's important to mention that you may have saved more than you currently possess if you have suffered any losses due to poor or untimely investing. The opposite may be true as well: you may have saved much less than 10% but scored well because you've been a savvy (or lucky) investor. Your savings score is really the amount you have *accumulated* in your lifetime up to this point. As you get into your savings plan in chapter 10, you'll learn how to make sure you consistently hit the 10% minimum target.

To use our navigation analogy again, if I asked you how you were doing on your trip to New York, and you told me you were in Colorado, we would have to review your original plan before we could evaluate your progress. If you had started in Louisiana, you'd be going backwards to end up in Colorado (getting further behind, like debt and overspending can cause). But if you started in California, then you appear to be making progress. We would also need to consider how long it took you to get there and when you want to arrive.

In the evaluation process, I offered you a few simple ways to evaluate how you are doing so you can begin to formulate the next steps of your financial journey. Some of these ways of evaluating are the exact criteria the lending industry uses (I know because I made these decisions on behalf of a major lender for many years); however, we used a different and higher standard here. They use criteria to evaluate whether you are credit worthy or a good risk but they don't have your best interest in mind; they have *their* best interest and profits in mind.

Although mine is a very fair evaluation system, this may have been a painful or unpleasant experience for you, but this awareness may be the jolt that gets you moving in a better direction at a faster pace. Unfortunately, most people don't (or won't) evaluate because they know that they are losing the game. They'd rather avoid that truth at all costs and keep doing what they're doing even though they know it won't get them anywhere. People who face the truth and use that experience and information to help themselves will move forward at a greater pace than ever before. I trust that you will use this moment as a pivotal point in your personal financial destiny.

Please know that it's not my place or anyone else's place to make a judgment about you, but rather to provide you with a reasonable and supportive measuring stick so you can evaluate yourself. I am simply offering some new guidelines and criteria to help you analyze your success in this critical area of your life. If you allow a bank, consumer lender, marketing institution, or merchant to decide whether you should spend or borrow more money, you will be "paying the man" for the rest of your life. If you don't believe me, just take a look at the root of the word *mortgage*. The great jurist Sir Edward Coke, who lived from 1552 to 1634, explained why the term *mortgage* comes from the Old French words *mort* ("dead") and *gage* ("pledge" or "challenge"). If you really look at this word, it means a challenge or pledge to the death. It seemed to Sir Edward that the word *mortgage* had to do with the doubtfulness of whether or not the mortgagor would ever pay the debt. It may be best to keep this in mind the next time you borrow money or refinance your home.

People I talk to one or two years after completing this evaluation process at my live or online seminars or via one-on-one coaching tell me that it was a very uncomfortable exercise for them, but that it provided the motivation to turn things around. The same was true for me when I did the process in October 1990. It took some honest answers to these specific questions to give me a sense of what I had done to my personal finances during those first 10 years after high school. I sincerely hope you will take a moment right now to acknowledge yourself for what you have just done. If you took the time to fill out the forms on the preceding pages, you have just accomplished more than most Americans in regard to personal

finances. Most people underestimate the power of awareness, and few people take the time to do this type of self-evaluation; therefore, they don't experience the level of financial success they truly deserve. I want to make sure you take a moment to give yourself a pat on the back.

If this was a painful or uncomfortable process, I also want to make sure you take a few moments right now to *make some new decisions* about how you're going to play the game called money. Remember that pain and frustration can be your friends if you embrace them and use them for your future success. When I did this process in 1990, I actually counted all the money I had spent on interest expense over the preceding few years. I became so angry and embarrassed about having done that to myself, but *that was the day I decided to master this part of my life* and share it with others so they could improve their lives, too.

Now that you've taken count and evaluated where you are, you're ready for the next process: to get out of debt as fast as possible. Before we get started I have a question for you: Are you ready for war? It's important to know up front that getting out of debt can be a battle that is not for the faint of heart.

I place debt among the greatest things to fear.

~ Thomas Jefferson

Chapter Three

Declaring Your Personal War on Debt

Recently on a flight from Chicago to Washington, D.C, I had the pleasure of sitting next to a U.S. Army colonel. After that first uncomfortable hello, we began to get acquainted. A striking African-American gentleman, he told me he was traveling home from his 20-year college reunion and that, after nearly 20 years of military service, he was currently attending "war school." As you can imagine, his comment intrigued me. It had never occurred to me that soldiers go to school to learn how to fight wars; I figured they gained that sort of practical knowledge from being in the field.

During our ensuing discussion, the colonel told me about his military career and what he was studying. He then asked what I did for a living. When I told him I was a financial coach and author who teaches the principles of financial success, emphasizing getting out and staying out of debt, he probed further and said, "So, tell me how you get out of debt." I gave him my best 30-second canned response and explained my CREDiT Method (details will follow in chapter 5). To my surprise, he replied, "That's just like what I am learning in school." By then I was bursting at the seams with curiosity. He explained that the strategy for efficiently and effectively getting out of debt is the same strategy used by the greatest military minds to elicit success in battles and war.

My travel companion held a book that summarized some of those great minds. They included Karl von Clausewitz, the writings of Sun Tzu on *The Art of War,* Frederick the Great, Napoleon Bonaparte, Theodore Roosevelt, and Confucius, to mention a few. The colonel explained that all of these men were considered great military strategists. Karl von Clausewitz, a legendary Prussian general, coined the term *massing of forces* and it is his principle of warfare that will be applied to eliminating your debt completely, attacking it with the best possible chance of a speedy victory.

Throughout this book, I use analogies of sports, games, health, travel, and weight loss. With the help of my new colonel friend, this time it's *war!* If you're going to get out of debt, you must wage war against the merchants, banks, credit companies, and marketing and advertising gurus. You must fight this war in specific battles against each and every debt you have right now. In this war, you are the general, which makes you responsible for setting up camp, assembling the troops, and mobilizing the army for victory.

A Crash Course in Victorious Warfare

Sun Tzu says that in war there are four ways to do battle and win, ranging from the simplest to the most difficult. Let's cover them one by one and then we'll apply them to the world of debt and borrowing.

The more than 2,000-year-old book by Sun Tzu says that "to subjugate the enemy's army *without doing battle* is the highest of excellence." This first and most elegant option relates to not overspending and *not getting into debt in the first place* by simply paying cash for your purchases. Attacking the enemies' plans with the mind-set of being debt free and not letting them get your hard-earned dollar is the best way to win the war.

The second best war strategy is to *attack alliances*. This relates to advertising and marketing companies as well as to the media who are doing everything they can to get you to spend your money. Marketing publications report that we see 50,000 images (messages) every day enticing us to buy something or at least to get our attention and begin building the desire. We must become highly sensitive to these assaults and stand guard at the door of our minds to avoid the unconscious actions of spending without understanding what we are doing and why.

The third and more difficult way to win a war is to *directly attack the army*. This strategy relates to banks and credit card companies and refers specifically to how you repay the money you owe. Do you fall victim to their amortization schedules and continue to borrow, or do you find a way to *accelerate the repayment schedule* to lower the total interest you pay and the time you're indebted to them? Chapter 5 includes a simple mathematical formula for repaying your debts to your ultimate advantage.

The fourth and most difficult method is *to attack a walled city*. This relates to multiple creditors, collection accounts and payments in arrears, late fees, and high interest rates. Banks and credit card companies build a "walled city" into their agreements and make it as hard as possible for you to win the war. Although this is the most difficult battle position, if you find yourself in this situation, you are now becoming a brilliant strategist; this chapter will help you create your plan for victory, no matter what the stakes.

I realize that this is a sensitive time to use a war analogy and, of course, there are many merchants who are not the enemy. Most businesses are simply trying to add value and supply a product and/or service, and the people who represent those businesses wholeheartedly believe in what they offer. In today's Western culture we all need to earn and spend money in order to survive, contribute to the economy, and improve the quality of our lives. However, merchants become the enemy when they willingly

do whatever it takes to get their product into your hands, whether or not you need it and can afford it. As discussed in chapter 1, these are often items that you may want but cannot afford in the moment. I'm still waiting for the day when a merchant says, "Well, Mr. and Mrs. Johnson, we'd love to sell you this couch but it appears you are in debt up to your eyeballs right now (based on this new set of measuring sticks), so how about this: you two go home, pay off all your credit cards, and then save the money. When you're ready to pay cash, we'll sell you the furniture." I know I'm being absurd, but you can't blame a guy for dreaming!

With that said, it's time to create a well-planned, strategic military campaign intended to bring about the speedy victory of being debt free and saving for your future independence. My goal for you in this chapter is to help you become a strategist and tactician of debt warfare, enabling you to defeat the enemy's assault against your hard-earned dollars (and in some cases, against your goals and dreams). The brilliant military strategist focuses on three aspects in which the battle will be fought:

- The *point where:* Your number one target for elimination
- The *time when:* Each month until it is gone
- The *numerical force:* The amount you pay each month

By using this triple determination you'll have a critical influence on the result of the combat and achieve your ultimate victory. You must become a master of these three elements to win the war. General Norman Schwarzkopf said, "Once the outcome has been determined, every other consideration and evaluation has to be made with this outcome in mind." Everything else that arises during your personal battle is simply a distraction. Are you ready? Are you prepared? Are you committed?

RECOGNIZING AND EVALUATING THE ENEMY

Realizing that you need to utilize the enemy's strengths and weaknesses to meet your objective (creating financial independence), you need to understand more about them. It's not my intent to bash big business in America, or any other country for that matter. In a sense, I too am one of them, creating and selling tools, books, coaching, and products. As is the case with most people in business, I truly believe in what I do and know I help people create a better quality of life. In my past career as a loan officer and collector, I was on the other side of the track. My goal now is purely to serve people in making their financial dreams come true.

I believe that only a small percentage of businesses and people deliberately try to scam, manipulate, or take advantage of others for their personal or corporate gain. Those organizations have built systems and invested billions of dollars to create, grow, and maximize their capacity to get us off the couch and on the phone, Internet, or down to their stores to make a purchase. What is their number one weapon? It's their ability to know what influences us at the deepest level and causes us to want something so badly that we'll do anything to get it. Think about it. They get us to spend money we have *yet to earn* and pay a *higher price* for it, all because of our desire to feed our need for the instant gratification they helped us create. Brilliant! What is their number one tool? It's the illusion that they are making things more affordable by breaking the cost into many small payments over a period of time. Then they become relentless predators, exploiting our strong desire for instant gratification. Why wait two years to take that dream vacation to Hawaii when you can put it all on your credit card and have it right now?

I recently purchased the Dell computer with which I typed this manuscript. Dell makes a great product, one that I trust and have enjoyed for the past seven years. I also have tremendous respect for the company's founder, chairman, and CEO, Michael Dell, and what he has

done in business. Improvements in technology occur rapidly, and sales messages are preprogrammed into my new machine. It seems like every time I boot up my computer, a message comes up asking me to download this and upgrade that. Of course, this makes it easy for me to click on a link; enter my credit card number; and get access to a newer, better, faster software program than the one included in my original purchase. I find myself asking, aren't they satisfied with the $2,369 I just spent? Where does it stop?

You must constantly remain aware of what's happening around you and stand guard at the door of your mind or you'll be spending more and more money before you even know it. Okay, I admit that I bit the bullet and spent eight dollars downloading some of my favorite songs from Dell's music Internet site. It's okay to make purchases, as long as you understand what you're doing and the long-term impact it will have on your financial plan and personal well-being. Just don't let yourself "impulse buy" your way into financial oblivion while these organizations profit big time.

I recently heard a song called "The Low Spark of High-Heeled Boys" (I have no idea what this title means but the lyrics are brilliant) by the band Traffic and sung by Steve Winwood. I had heard the song many times before but this time I listened more carefully. The lyrics sum up what I've been speaking about in these past few paragraphs:

The sentence you're paying is too high-priced
When you're living beyond all your means,
And the man in the suit has just bought a new car
From the profit he made on your dreams.

THE THREE MOST DAMAGING WORDS TO YOUR FINANCIAL PLAN

The three most dangerous and destructive words to your financial plan are *low monthly payments*. Since questions determine what you focus on, organizations get you to focus on ridiculously low payments that anyone can afford by getting you to ask yourself whether you can afford the low monthly payment? In sales, this is referred to as *reducing it to the ridiculous*. For example: "You can have this new refrigerator for the price of a cup of coffee each day," or "This insurance policy will cost you only 75 cents per day. Isn't your family worth that?"

Merchants and the lending industry attempt to hypnotize us into believing that the consequences of our choices are minimal because of the low amount we have to commit to each month. Little is said about the *total cost* of these time payments. With larger purchases like homes and autos, the law requires that buyers receive a document called a Truth in Lending Disclosure, which reveals the total cost of their borrowing decision, but I don't think the lending institutions want us to read it. Since the rules right now are broad in scope, many types of loans are excluded from these disclosures. At some point in the future, the Truth in Lending Act (TILA) and Regulation Z will need to be modified to add this type of disclosure to monthly credit card statements. It would look something like this:

TABLE 3.1 SAMPLE CREDIT CARD DISCLOSURE

Balance Owed	Interest Rate	Monthly Payment	Years to Payoff	Cost to Borrow	Total Payback
$3,500	15%	$70*	28.2	$5,290	**$8,790**

*Based on a 2% minimum monthly payment

Wouldn't seeing this information on your credit card statement motivate you to pay back your debt more quickly? Again, lenders want you to focus on the lowest common denominator rather than the *ultimate consequence* of your decision to buy now. They are also eroding your plan— or in most cases *your lack of a plan*—for financial independence. Now you can step back and decide which merchants are your enemies and which ones you want to do business with. When you make a decision, you support your ultimate goal of personal financial independence rather than falling into the traps the lenders have set. This is an all-out war for your precious cash. You can't and won't win the war by following the lending industry's plan instead of your own.

THE LENDING INDUSTRY'S FORMULA FOR BUSINESS SUCCESS

The lenders' secret ingredient lies in a loan's *amortization* (how long it takes you to pay it back). Remember the root of the word *mortgage* again: it comes from *mort,* meaning death. If you throw everything I'm saying out the window, fail to follow through on anything in this book, and remember just one thing, remember this: It's not how much you owe or even the interest rate that makes the biggest difference; it's how you *repay* that has the biggest impact. Remember that an APR is an annual percentage rate but most things you buy are not amortized over one year, they are amortized in two years or as many as 40 and 50 years for mortgages and credit cards.

Here's the lending industry's formula:

Amount Financed x APR + Compounding + <u>Amortization</u> = Big Profits

---

A close friend of mine is a certified public accountant. While discussing his mortgage loan, I explained that he and his wife should pay it off as fast as possible to save money. He took the position that at an interest rate of 5.75%, his mortgage was "cheap money" that he could use to invest elsewhere since he had such a great interest rate and a tax advantage.

My friend had borrowed $465,000 for 30 years and his payments were approximately $2,700 per month. Since he had recently refinanced, the loan was brand-new and only about $490 went to the principal, for a total of about 18% ($490 divided by $2,700).

I asked my friend, "If you're paying 82% of your monthly payment toward interest, how is that 5.75%?" Dumfounded, he said, "I never thought of it like that." I explained that he *should* think of it this way since this is the reality. Then he said, "But it's tax deductible."

I asked my friend, "Which would you rather have in your pocket, $70 or $30?" Of course he chose the $70. I went on to explain that the mortgage interest tax deduction is another way for lenders to keep you in debt by getting you focused on the wrong objective. The way they propose it confuses people in regard to their focus and goals. I appeal to you to look at it this way:

Scenario 1 (the way lenders want you to look at it):

You earn $100 income	All $100 is applied to mortgage interest	You receive a 30% tax deduction*	= $30 net in your pocket

Scenario 2 (the way I want you to look at it from now on):

You earn $100 income	You deposit it in your savings account	You pay $30 in taxes*	= $70 net in your pocket

*Assuming a 30% tax bracket

Lenders want you to focus on the $30 you are "saving" but let me ask you a question. Is your desired outcome to save on your taxes or is it to become financially independent as fast as possible? I sincerely hope you picked the latter. Of course I understand the need to get a mortgage, since not many people have hundreds of thousands of dollars lying around for a home purchase. I'm not disputing having a mortgage to leverage your buying power and help you get into a home or purchase multiple properties for investment purposes. I certainly am not arguing the benefit of a tax break, either. I just don't want you to make it your ultimate objective. A tax break should be a *temporary benefit and nothing more.* What I am disputing is being hypnotized by the banks and lending industry to pay back the loan as agreed and buy into the false illusion that you're getting a great deal. We tend to think that interest rates are inexpensive because we're comparing or contrasting them with higher lending rates for autos, credit cards, and personal loans, especially during markets like the one that exists as I write this book, when mortgage rates are near their all-time low.

Banks and credit card companies will ask you for only 2–3% of your balance each month. Do you think they do it because they're caring organizations that want people to have more money for themselves? Hardly! They do it because they know that if they extend your credit as long as they can and ask you for only the minimum amount, it will take you more than 30 years to pay off the balance and, because of the amortization schedule, the loan will cost you thousands—even tens of thousands—in interest payments. Trust me, they don't have your best interest in mind; they have *their own* best interest in mind. Only recently has legislation been passed requiring banks to request 4% as a minimum payment because of the damage the lower amount is causing.

WHAT IS THE SOLUTION?

To win this war, you must control your mind and thought process and understand that you really want financial independence. You must stay focused on that goal and consistently ask deliberate questions that will support your objectives. You must also evaluate the impact of your decisions. When it comes to your personal finances you can't afford to be on autopilot. You have to be deliberate about what you want, why you want it, and how you're going to get it.

Part 3 of this book will take you through a short process to help you clarify what you want and discover what it will take to become financially independent. Most people don't make the effort to invest in themselves, which is why people are getting poorer while big business in America gets richer. *No one will care more about your money than you will.* It is therefore time to focus on making the intelligent choices that will lead to a prosperous future.

If you find yourself suddenly wanting something that was not in your original plan for the year, quarter, or month, you must stop and ask yourself four questions:

1. Is this something I want or something I really need? Did this want/need come from within me or was I captivated by merchants and marketing specialists?

2. Have I planned for this expense so I can pay cash?

3. Have I thought about how this will impact my goals for the month or year?

4. What's a better way to make this purchase so I can stay on my plan? (For example, could I wait another month or year or purchase when the item is on sale, out of season, or not as popular?)

This past Christmas my wife asked if I wanted anything specific from Santa Claus (she looks very cute in that red outfit). I had admired a jacket in a catalogue but I hesitated because it was quite expensive. She told me she didn't care and asked me to show her the jacket. I did, but only after she promised that if she were going to buy it, she would wait because I knew it would go on sale the day after Christmas. I told her I would rather receive it the next week at a reduced price. Sure enough, I went on the Web site the day after Christmas and the jacket was 25% off.

If you can interrupt your own spending pattern and begin to ask these questions before every purchase, you'll discover a power that all successful and financially sound people have. *It's the power of self-direction and deliberate action toward a well-thought-out goal and financial plan.* We'll talk in much more detail about spending smart in part 2 of this book.

Your Formula for Winning the War

While doing battle with your existing debts, you must take their amortization schedules out of the formula and turn the compounding table in your favor to ultimately win the war. Your new formula looks like this:

Clear Purpose/Goals + Savings + Planned Spending x <u>Compounded Growth</u> = Financial Independence

---

Your initial battle will be more difficult because you have to deploy your army (dollars) in three directions:

- Toward your *monthly expenses* (both fixed and discretionary). This also includes any amounts for long-term saving purposes.

- Toward your *current debts* to pay them down.

- Toward *future expenses* so you don't get further into debt or keep your balances where they are.

Of course, once you totally eliminate your debts (including your mortgage), your only focus will be on your monthly expenses and staying out of debt. This is your *saving to spend* or cookie jar plan. I may not be completely finished ranting about the lending industry, but for now I want to get you started on your plan. Here we go.

Nothing is particularly hard if you divide it into small jobs.

~ Ray Kroc, Founder of
McDonald's Restaurants

CHAPTER FOUR

Three Types of Debt and Five Sources of Borrowing

In his groundbreaking book, *How to Get Out of Debt, Stay Out of Debt, and Live Prosperously*, Jerrold Mundis defines debt in three classifications: reasonable, problematic, and compulsive.

Reasonable debt typically includes purchases used for investments or for tools that help you be more productive. Reasonable debt allows you to leverage your money to create a greater good or a greater return on your investment. I would be a fool to say that all debt is bad. Once you understand the fundamental principle that you can't have financial freedom without debt freedom, and the fact that most credit purchases will take you further away from your goal of financial independence, then you can evaluate certain borrowing (leveraging) scenarios as a part of the process of becoming financially solvent.

Problematic debt comes from telling yourself you need something that you actually just want. You may tell yourself you have a plan ("I'll pay this off when I get my raise or bonus"). In truth, unless you pay for the purchase in full before the next statement arrives from your bank, you will incur an interest expense that takes you further from financial independence.

Compulsive debt is usually marked as spending that comes more frequently, adds to your problem, involves no plan, and permeates other areas of your life (such as your health, relationships, and happiness).

Compulsive debt is the type that occurs when you're walking down the street, you see a new outfit in a store window, and you finance the purchase without any regard to the consequences. The more important issue with compulsive spending is that it may be tied to emotional issues and a void you're trying to fill in your life. Having been born with a birth defect, I understand the dynamic: something is missing in your life and you get a temporary emotional hit by spending money. Believe me, there's no way to win in this situation. Happiness is an inside job and no purchase you make will have a permanent impact on your self-esteem; such purchases are guaranteed to be temporary. To use our weight analogy again, overeating for the purpose of feeling better will only make you fatter.

Adding to Mr. Mundis's work, I have listed five sources of borrowing and where they fit within his model of the three types of debt:

1. **Home mortgages and auto loans:** These purchases are typically considered reasonable debt because they can become tools for investment or production. However, they can fall into the categories of problematic or even compulsive debt if they are abused. For example, a second mortgage could be problematic and a third mortgage could be compulsive. Also, they often include the issues of making sure your principal and payments are not excessive (such as buying a Ferrari when a Toyota will do the trick) and avoiding sub-prime lenders (lenders who charge you more, in many cases due to a poor credit score).

2. **Business and education loans:** These types of borrowing fall into the category of reasonable debt because they are investments by nature. However, frequency and overall circumstances must be considered because they can become problematic as well.

3. **Credit cards and retail installment loans:** Unless you paid your balance each month it would be hard to justify these types of debt as anything better than problematic.

4. **Personal loans, medical bills, and IRS/back taxes:** At best these types of debts are problematic because they typically come from a lack of planning and preparedness. Even medical bills, which can be unforeseen or arise from emergencies, fall into the category of problematic debt if you can't pay them promptly, put them on a credit card, or make other payment arrangements that result in interest or penalties.

5. **Paycheck loans, loan sharks, and sub-prime borrowing:** There's only one way to describe this type of debt and that is compulsive. If you're using these services it's typically for day-to-day expenses. At this point you aren't even living paycheck to paycheck.

A DOLLAR IS NOT A DOLLAR

The following analogy illustrates an important dynamic that takes place every time you send money to your bank or finance company. I point this out to show you the *real impact* borrowing has on your financial plan and the *real cost* of interest expense. The expense of your dollar toward interest is not a dollar out of your pocket; it is actually *two dollars or more.*

Imagine that you and I are standing side by side in the middle of a staircase. At the top of the stairs is our ultimate financial destiny, and at the bottom are financial despair and poverty. When I receive income and I invest one dollar into a basic money market or savings account, I get to take *one step up.* When you receive a dollar and use it to pay down your principal balance, you get to stay on the same stair, but when your dollar goes to interest, late fees, or penalties, you now have to take *one step down.* In this scenario with me taking one step up and you taking one step down, how many steps are we apart? Not one but two! That one dollar you paid toward interest has really cost you two because it's now a dollar you did not save or invest and it's gone forever. Every dollar that goes to banks

and credit card companies in the form of an interest payment is costing you two dollars or more from your dreams and goals.

Look at your statements and see what you paid last month on your credit card bill. Was it $20, $30, maybe $50 or $100? Just double that amount and that's what you're paying every month toward *not* achieving your goals. Instead, imagine investing that dollar and watching it grow. Now the gap is more than two dollars. The amounts can be extraordinary when you become a successful investor who *never* pays for interest or does so only when it leverages more investments or your productivity.

SIX OPTIONS FOR GETTING OUT OF DEBT AND THE UPSIDE/DOWNSIDE OF EACH

Before I introduce you to my fail-proof system for getting out of debt fast, let's take a brief look at all of your options for getting out of debt. I strongly believe that the person with the most options always wins. The important thing to remember is that even though each option has a proven upside (which is hyped in all of the marketing materials for each option), there's typically a downside as well. My CREDiT Method incorporates the positives of each while avoiding the negative consequences. If you're considering one or more of these options, you need to know the whole truth before you act. Let's look at them one by one and then you can begin creating your plan for total debt elimination.

1. Debt Consolidation and/or Real Estate Refinance

This very popular choice is done by qualifying for one or more larger loans and then paying off many creditors simultaneously by wrapping their loans into the higher-balance loan, credit card, or mortgage.

Upside
- It lowers your interest rate in some cases (especially on real estate refinance), depending on timing and market conditions.

- It lowers the number of creditors and payments you have to pay each month.

- It lowers your monthly payments, which can relieve you from high payments that exceed your budget.

- Mortgage interest can now be applied to reduce your taxable income.

Downside

- Sometimes you pay a loan-processing fee or higher interest rate, depending on your credit history or market conditions and timing.

- It can create a false sense of debt reduction because there's only one bill instead of the many you had prior to the consolidation.

- In most cases, when you lower your payment, you increase the amount of time you're paying on your debt, thus creating yet another false sense of success.

- You lose positive equity in your home investment.

- You may not qualify for a loan or may have to give up collateral or get a cosigner.

- Unless the problem is cured at the source (overspending) you'll charge your balances back up and wind up with the bigger consolidated balance plus all the new debt payments.

- You can wind up losing your home or personal property to foreclosure.

2. Bankruptcy

Bankruptcy is a legally declared inability or impairment of your ability to repay creditors and debts. When you're unable to repay your debts due to a sudden loss of income, mismanaged spending, or being

unprepared for family or medical emergencies, you have a legal right to declare bankruptcy protection through the federal court system.

We'll evaluate the two most popular forms of bankruptcy as defined by the U.S. Federal Courts. The first is Chapter 7, known as a liquidation or straight bankruptcy. The second is Chapter 13, known as a wage-earner's plan.

Chapter 7 is the most common form of bankruptcy. It is a liquidation proceeding in which the debtor's non-exempt assets, if any, are sold by the Chapter 7 trustee and the proceeds distributed to creditors according to priorities established in the Bankruptcy Code.

Upside

- You can virtually eliminate all of your unsecured debt in a matter of days.

- This form helps you protect yourself from harassing creditors.

- You will be able to keep most of your possessions.

- You can remove and discharge liens from secured assets (like a home).

- You can alleviate stress that comes with the inability to repay.

- You can reaffirm certain debts to keep the asset.

- Chapter 7 bankruptcy can help you create a fresh start if utilized properly.

- It does not completely eliminate you from the credit market. Usually you can get back in within one year (this could also be considered a downside).

Downside

- Knowing you did not fulfill your obligations can create a lack of self-esteem.

- It will create poor credit ratings for 10 years.

- It will become a matter of your public record indefinitely.

- It will not create relief from secured debts.

- It can make future borrowing more difficult (which may not be so bad).

- It can force you to live on a cash basis (which, again, may not be so bad).

- You'll have attorney fees and legal costs (anywhere from $300 to $1,500).

- You rely on someone else to handle this (and you may get bad advice).

- You're passing responsibility to the legal system.

- You may not qualify (due to income limitations, e.g., you earn too much).

- You may lose secured assets to liquidation (e.g., furniture, car, etc.).

- It may not eliminate certain taxes (less than three years old).

- It may not eliminate education loans.

- It will most likely mean higher interest rates for you in the future.

Chapter 13 bankruptcy is a repayment plan for individuals with regular income and unsecured debt. The debtor keeps his or her property and makes regular payments to the Chapter 13 trustee out of future income to pay creditors over time (three to five years). Repayment in Chapter 13 can range from 10% to 100% depending on the debtor's income and the makeup of the debt. Chapter 13 also provides a mechanism for individuals to prevent foreclosures and repossessions while catching up on their secured debts. In Chapter 13, the debtor retains ownership and possession of all of his or her assets.

Upside

- It can be used when you're behind on a mortgage or other secured debt.

- You can protect yourself from harassing creditors.

- You will be able to keep most of your possessions.

- It can alleviate stress that comes with the inability to repay.

- It can remove and discharge liens from secured assets (like a home).

- You have a court-controlled repayment plan that your creditors must allow.

- Certain debts that cannot be discharged in Chapter 7 can be discharged in Chapter 13.

- It can help if you have a sudden loss of income (from an injury, illness, or job loss) but are now back working and, although behind, have the ability to pay.

- It does not completely eliminate you from the credit market. Usually you can get back in within one year (this could also be considered a downside).

- Paying back at least a portion of your debts (as determined by the courts) can create a sense of pride.

- It lets your attorneys handle all of the legal issues and communication with creditors.

Downside

- Payments can be deducted from your payroll so your employer will know you filed.

- It will create poor credit ratings for at least seven years.

- It will become a matter of your public record indefinitely.

- It can make future borrowing more difficult (which may not be so bad).

- It can force you to live on a cash basis (which, again, may not be so bad).

- You'll have attorney fees and legal costs (anywhere from $300 to $1,500).

- You have to rely on someone else to handle it (and you may get bad advice).

- You're passing responsibility to the legal system.

- You may not qualify (income limitations, e.g., you earn too much).

- You may lose secured assets (e.g., furniture, car, etc).

- It may not eliminate certain taxes (less than three years old).

- It will most likely mean higher interest rates for you in the future.

3. The Rollover, Power Down, or Snowball Method

The foundation of this strategy comes from the massing of forces military strategy mentioned in chapter 3. This efficient and cost-saving strategy helps you get out of debt by using a time-tested campaign that puts mathematics on your side. Think of your debt situation as a war made up of many battles (individual creditors and balances). You continue to pay the minimum monthly payment on all of your debts but one. This battle becomes your number one target for elimination. You gather as many troops (dollars) as possible in addition to the minimum payment due and consistently apply them to this debt until it is gone. Then you take the minimum monthly payment plus the additional amount you were paying and apply them to your next debt in line (your new number one target) until it is gone. You continue in this manner until all your debts are

gone, including mortgages if you have them. The key to this strategy is to keep paying the minimum monthly payment amounts from your terminated accounts toward your existing debts.

Most quality organizations that teach you how to get out of debt use this method. Although the principles and strategies are the same, you'll hear different terms to describe the same philosophy and process. It has widely been referred to as the snowball method because, like a snowball that gets bigger and bigger as it rolls down a hill, your payment grows as you move down the line on your debts. When you get to your final creditor and balance, you still pay the same amount as when you started your program (or more if you have increased your income and/or cut expenses) but you direct it toward fewer debts.

Upside

- It puts the majority of your focus on one debt at a time.

- It makes debt freedom a priority.

- You eliminate your smallest debts first, lowering the number of creditors you pay each month as quickly as possible.

- You don't need much additional money other than your minimum payments to get started.

- You get an immediate sense of accomplishment by eliminating your smallest debts first. This creates positive momentum and applies the law of attraction—that popular phrase that means whatever you focus on, you attract into your life—in the right direction.

- You increase your net worth each month.

- Doing this on your own gives you a sense of pride and total personal responsibility.

- You pay the same amount each month until you're completely out of debt.

Downside

- It may postpone higher interest rates for smaller balances but in most cases the overall financial impact can be minimal.

- You're instructed to pay off certain bills first (based on lowest balance), not taking into consideration your own personal motivation.

- It has an impact on your lifestyle because you continue to pay the same amount (even though your debt payments are reduced over time) until you're out of debt.

4. Chasing Lower Interest Rates

This means continuing to obtain lower interest rates, usually through introductory rates or special offers. The goal is to pay off higher-rate accounts with lower rates via bank and credit company promotions.

Upside

- You can receive low interest rates, thereby increasing the amount of money paid to the principal balance, albeit for a short time (usually 30–180 days).

Downside

- You spend valuable time filling out credit card applications and moving money around.

- You need to constantly focus on when the interest rates adjust upward so you know when to repeat the process.

- Terms and conditions can change your interest rate upon any type of default or late payment.

- It requires a lot of effort for very little reward and takes your focus away from your real objective, which is to get out of debt.

- In many cases, if you're late even once, you can be subjected to extremely high rates.

5. Debt Relief, Reduction, and Negotiating Services

This fifth strategy involves retaining organizations to manage the process of lowering your debt burden by bartering with credit companies on your behalf. While having a fair amount of good intent, these organizations play off of your own lack of education and personal responsibility.

Upside

- You can lower the balances owed or the interest rates through negotiation.

- You might make one payment to a counselor who pays all your bills for you.

- The counselor can get harassing creditors to stop ringing your phone.

- Banks and credit companies may work better with a professional than with you.

Downside

- Debt reduction in excess of $600 can be added to your income (shown on a 1099 form) and you can wind up owing taxes if you have a positive net worth.

- Many of these companies are scams, collecting high and/or hidden fees and charges.

- Failing to take responsibility for your actions can create a lack of pride and self-esteem.

- Plans created for you are not always in your best interest.

- Their education services make you a victim, fallen to outside forces rather than understanding where the real problem starts (overspending).

- Lack of follow-up service can keep you uninformed about what is happening.

- Your credit rating suffers because you are instructed by the negotiator not to pay while they work with your creditor.

- Student loans are federal loans and cannot be negotiated.

- You will lose the privilege of further credit from your former lenders (which may not be so bad).

6. Run and Hide

This is simply the "strategy" of running away from your responsibilities and hoping they go away without being repaid. Some people accomplish this by going AU (address unknown) on their creditors until the creditor writes the debt off as a loss and gives up trying to collect.

Upside

- It provides relief from payments (although most likely this will only be temporary).

Downside

- Your credit rating will be destroyed.

- Your creditors will most likely find you.

- This "strategy" does not relieve you from your debts.

- It could be viewed as a cowardly way to handle your responsibilities and will put a negative energy into your financial universe (what comes around, goes around).

Now that you know your options and the upside and downside of each, let me ask you a question: Do you have the soul of a slave or do you have the soul of a free person? Do you want to be a slave to the big businesses that want to grab every dollar they can from your hopes and dreams of being financially free or do you want to break the chains that hold you in slavery to your debt burden each month and each year? If you want to break free, we'll now create your five-minute plan for total debt freedom. Let's get started!

If a man has within him the soul of a slave will he not become one no matter what his birth?

~ George Clason,
The Richest Man in Babylon

CHAPTER FIVE

The CREDiT Method for Total Debt Elimination

In 1986 while working as a waiter in a Southern California restaurant, I met a man who appeared to be very successful. He was an older, charming, and unassuming real estate investor named Campbell Fraser. Rather than reinventing the wheel, I wanted to learn from him by modeling, the concept we discussed in chapter 1, so I invited him to lunch and asked for his advice. Mr. Fraser suggested that I read three books: *Think and Grow Rich* by Napoleon Hill, *The Success System That Never Fails* by W. Clement Stone, and *The Richest Man in Babylon* by George Clason. Because I wanted what this man had, I marched right out of that restaurant and immediately purchased all three.

In *The Richest Man in Babylon,* Clason tells the story of Debasir, a simple camel trader from Babylon, which at the time was the richest city in the world. A free man who became a slave, Debasir fought to regain his personal freedom and create the life of his dreams. Although the book had been written more than 80 years earlier by a man I'd never met, it was my story as well and it inspired my method of getting out of debt fast and for the least amount of interest expense possible (the true killer of your financial success). If you've become a slave to your debt burden, this can become your story of triumph, too.

Debasir the camel trader liked expensive things. Because he consistently spent more than he earned, he developed the habit of borrowing from different merchants in the city to finance his bigger-than-salary lifestyle. As he grew further and further behind, he one day realized that he had created a mess of his finances and that, not being a resourceful man, he would have to flee Babylon to escape the negative situation he had created for himself. Leaving his wife, he used the run-and-hide method to get out of debt, which typically does not work. While running from his responsibilities he came across a band of thieves who befriended him and brought him into their misguided ways of the world. One night while planning to rob some local merchants, Debasir and his band of friends were caught, arrested, and sold into slavery.

Working as a slave, Debasir had much time to reflect upon his mistakes and errors in judgment. Full of regret, he wished for a chance to make things right, but what could he do? One of his master's wives took a liking to him and knew that he was a good man who had made some bad choices. She challenged him to evaluate his current conditions, what he wanted for his life, and his *resolve* to turn things around. (Sound like a familiar person in your life?) One night while meeting privately with his newfound friend, Debasir spoke of his desires to break out of slavery, return to Babylon, and make everything right in his life again. His friend told him that she would be willing to help him escape and that she had thought up a plan to do so. Fearing what might happen should he escape, the rugged desert that lay between him and his goal of freedom, and the uncertainty of his return to Babylon, he kindly told her that he could not accept her offer. But she asked him a critical question that changed everything that night. She asked, "Debasir, have you the soul of a slave or have you the soul of a free man?" He started to cry and he convincingly replied, "I do have the soul of a free man." With this newfound decision of who he was and his refusal to settle for less than he could be, Debasir decided to take her up on her offer to help him escape. After many days of crossing the desert and nearly dying from lack of food and water, he reached his beloved Babylon. With a new resolve and a well-thought-out plan he began to take immediate action.

The CREDiT Method

My CREDiT Method was designed to get you out of debt as fast as possible and help you define a *compelling* plan for total debt freedom in as little as five minutes. With this five-step process, you can create a detailed plan for total debt elimination, including your mortgage if you own a home. With the proper calculator, you'll be able to see exactly how much money and how many payments (in months and years) you'll save by following this time-tested system. In many cases you can take tens if not hundreds of thousands of your hard-earned dollars and several years or even decades off of a plan that has you making minimum payments.

The CREDiT Method is the combined result of two profound teachings I've been exposed to in my many years of coaching people on their personal finances. The first is the book I have been speaking of, *The Richest Man in Babylon*. The second is the concept of massing of force, which means winning a war one battle (debt) at a time.

The story of the camel trader inspired me to create my very simple system to eliminate debt, including mortgage debt, in a time frame that seems impossible to most people. I can assure you, if you follow this system it will work. With a few additions relevant to today's world, the mathematical formula and strategy for getting out of debt fast is the same massing of forces war strategy used by Debasir and millions of people since his time, whether they knew it or not. It has been written about in other books on getting out of debt (and missing from many) and it is the core of my CREDiT Method, which is simply an acronym for the five steps you take to make this plan work for you. After a preparation process,

it will take you only five minutes to go through each step and create a compelling plan that will break you free of the slavery of debt once and for all. Let's take it letter by letter, step by step, and then we'll build *your* plan together.

C = Capture

Like Debasir did on his clay tablets, you must first *capture* all of your debts onto paper. (I have provided a worksheet for you in the following pages or you can use a software program like Quicken, Microsoft Money, or even Microsoft Excel.) You started this process in chapter 2 during the Take Count process. You simply need to capture four things:

- Who you owe
- How much you owe
- The interest rate
- The minimum monthly payment (be sure to use the *minimum* payment listed on your bill or statement and not any other amount)

R = Resolve

This second critical step provides the emotion to help you make it across your desert when things get difficult and to sustain your goal over time. Merely being interested in accomplishing debt freedom won't make it happen. You must *resolve* that it *must* happen and that *you* will make it happen. No one will do it for you—no bankruptcy lawyer, mortgage consolidation expert, debt counselor, or family member. You and only you can make this happen.

Three resolutions need to happen at this point:

- You must resolve to *get out of debt as fast as possible* using the massing of forces strategy I've outlined for you.

- You must resolve to *stay out of debt forever*. You don't want to "lose the weight" only to gain it back again, and the simple process outlined in part 2 of this book will help you achieve this.

- You must resolve to *help others do the same*. What you talk about becomes more exciting. Simply sharing your goals and encouraging others—your friends, family, and/or business associates—to do the same will help you stay focused and keep you on track. You may even enjoy knowing that you may have made a difference in the lives of others.

You must write out a statement of *all the reasons* why you must get out of debt now and all that it is costing you to be enslaved by your creditors. You must write about how it will feel to be debt free and vividly imagine the lifestyle you'll have when you achieve this deserved goal. I can tell you without hesitation that *reasons come first*. If you aren't compelled to accomplish this, you won't follow through. Period!

E = Execute

The most effective and efficient way to attack your debt is by using the massing of forces war strategy. It's known in the financial arena as the snowball or power down method. No matter what you call it, this simply means paying the minimum monthly payment on all of your debts but one, and that one becomes your number one target for elimination. That one debt will receive the majority of your forces (your dollars) to eliminate the enemy (your debt principal balance) while you fight the other battles with the minimum payments necessary. Later in this chapter you'll find four criteria to help you decide which debt will become your number one target.

Di = Decide and invest

Two critical decisions need to be made at this point. First, you must *decide* on an amount that you will pay toward eliminating your debt, over

and above the sum of your minimum payments. You can decide on a single dollar amount (e.g., $50, $200, or $500), or you can choose a percentage of your income. (In my seminars and coaching, I recommend that a minimum of 20% of your gross monthly income goes to pay your debt burden.) This amount will be known as your Debt Elimination Accelerator or DEA Factor™, and it will be the basis of accelerating your plan to debt freedom.

Other than resolving to eliminate your debt burden, there may not be a more important decision than coming up with the DEA Factor. Continuing with our war analogy, Sun Tzu wrote that *superiority in numbers* is the most important factor in the end result of combat; it must be sufficiently great to counterbalance all the other cooperating circumstances (interest rate, balance owed, amortization schedule, penalties, and late fees). The greatest possible number of troops (your money) should be brought into action at this decisive point. The key to this strategy is that you pay the same amount every month until the end of your plan, even after you start eliminating debts. In part 3 of this book we'll take a hard look at your entire spending plan to make sure this number is sufficient and sustainable throughout your journey to debt freedom and ultimately financial independence.

The second decision in this step is the decision to *invest.* This step is simple and really takes no time. Make a decision *right now* to invest toward your debt any additional money you acquire, including bonuses, cash gifts, inheritance, overtime pay, tax refunds, money from second jobs, garage sales, etc. You must make a commitment in advance to invest any and all additional monies. If these inflows are predictable (such as an upcoming bonus), make a commitment *in advance* to apply them to your debt before you squander the money on miscellaneous expenses. This doesn't mean you can't have fun with your additional money; it just means that you plan to invest the majority (at least 50–80% of your net) toward accelerating your plan to get completely out of debt. I believe this intention can even attract more money into your life. Your commitment evokes the unspoken belief that you are worthy of more money because you know how to handle and invest it wisely. There are many stories and examples of people whose financial lives shifted after they made their positive intentions clear. This phenomenon is also referred to as the law of attraction. On the flip side, remember, George Clason in *The Richest Man in Babylon* tells us that "gold [money] avoids those unwise in its use." Be wise and watch your financial world open up!

T = Terminate

The final step in the CREDiT Method is to stick to your plan and terminate one debt at a time (the one you select as your number one target). The key is this: when you terminate a debt, you transfer the sum of the *minimum monthly payment of that expired debt* plus the *DEA Factor* toward the next debt in line (your new number one target). This creates a snowball effect—the amount keeps growing as you move down the line and eliminate each debt. For a visual example, please see the sample plan later in this chapter (table 5.2).

It's critical to continue to pay the *same amount* each month (the sum of all your minimum payments plus your DEA Factor) or more until your debts are gone. This includes your mortgage(s). As you continue to pay down your other revolving debts, the minimum payments will decrease. This won't be significant at first but over time it can add up, so make sure you look at this and raise your DEA Factor accordingly.

USE THE CREDiT METHOD TO CREATE YOUR PLAN

Let's create a rough draft of your plan right now. You'll have to write it out and then rewrite it one final time to make it complete, clear, and compelling. Make sure you gather all necessary documents (loan and credit card statements, mortgage info, etc.) so you can start with the most

accurate information. After you gather your documents, it will take only five minutes or less to go through each step of the CREDiT Method and create your plan.

Step 1: Capture

Capture all your debt information onto the following form. Be sure to list everything.

TABLE 5.1 DEBT INFORMATION

Creditor/ Lender	Total Balance Owed	APR Interest Rate	Minimum Mo. Pmt.
	$	%	$
	$	%	$
	$	%	$
	$	%	$
	$	%	$
	$	%	$
	$	%	$
	$	%	$
	$	%	$
	$	%	$
	$	%	$
	$	%	$
Total:	$		$

Step 2: Resolve

Take a focused five minutes and brainstorm all the reasons you must get out of debt now. Be sure to list what it will mean to you, your family, and anyone else who may be affected. Also describe what your life will be like when you are totally debt free and how it will feel to achieve that goal.

Resolve (Why must you get out of debt now?):

_____

_____

_____

_____

_____

_____

Step 3: Execute

Take five minutes to execute the massing of forces strategy by determining which debt will be your number one target for elimination. There are four criteria for making this decision. Remember, your objective is to get out of debt as fast as possible for the least amount of interest expense possible. Using the four strategic ways to approach your elimination plan, your goal is to create a hierarchy that gives you the maximum mathematical advantage for elimination.

1. *Pay down the debt with the highest interest rate:*

   This option makes the most sense mathematically because higher-interest accounts do the most damage each month. I recommend that you use this as your primary criterion, but there may be reasons the following options might work for you and your personal situation. If you choose another option as your first criterion, I would certainly recommend that you use this as the criterion for choosing your number two target for debt reduction.

2. *Pay down the debt with the lowest balance:*

   I recommend this approach because smaller balances will be eliminated more quickly. Seeing debt disappear can give you an immediate sense of accomplishment. This approach also expedites the snowball effect by moving the monthly payment from that debt plus your DEA Factor to your number two target.

3. *Pay down the debt with the fewest payments left:*

   This approach has benefits similar to option number two. For example, if you have a car payment with eight payments left and with your DEA Factor it will be gone in three to four months, making this your number one target could be the best option for you. The only deterrent to choosing this option is if you have a debt that has only a few payments left and has a very low interest rate (such as an education loan). In that case, you may want to place this lower on your list and go after the higher-interest loans first.

4. *Pay down the balance you're most motivated to pay off:*

   This could be the most powerful option for some people. Review the debts you captured in step one and ask yourself this question: *Is there a debt on this list that, for strong emotional reasons, I am most motivated to pay off now?* Remember, the more reasons you have, the more likely you are to follow through. A sense of accomplishment, regardless of the interest rate or balance owed, can be quite motivating. I once coached a good friend who was in the middle of a divorce. He'd been left with a substantial balance of approximately $11,000 on his wife's credit card. Needless to say, that became his number one target for many emotional reasons. (An added bonus was that it happened to be among the higher interest rates as well.)

From these four criteria, decide which debt will become your number one target and write it below. If you know right now which debt will become your next target, go ahead and list it as your number two target.

Target #	Lender
My #1 Target	_____
My #2 Target	_____

Step 4: Decide and invest

Now take five minutes and come up with a specific amount (either a dollar figure or a percentage of your gross monthly income) in addition to your minimum monthly payments that you will devote solely to your debt elimination plan and specifically to your number one target. Don't think about the "how" here, just decide on a number you believe you can commit to each month. Decide on the amount to become your DEA Factor.

Each month I will commit to $_____ on top of my minimum debt payments to use as my DEA Factor.

Take a moment and also set your intention to *invest* any additional monies throughout the year toward accelerating your plan. If you already know of money that will be coming in, maybe in the form of a bonus or tax refund, for example, make a note of it here.

I also commit to *invest* $_____ in one lump some at some point in the year.

Part 2 of this book is devoted to looking at your expenses one by one and making some cuts where possible. After completing this exercise, you may want to come back to this part of the process and beef up your DEA Factor if possible. Remember, the more troops (money) you send into battle, the faster the victory.

Step 5: Terminate

Now take five more minutes to write up the final draft of your plan on one piece of paper. You can also download a spreadsheet from my Web site at ww.5MinuteDebtSolution.com that will calculate these elements for you and show *how much you will save* and precisely *when you will be completely out of debt.* You can also access the necessary calculators so you can see how long (time payments in months) it will take you to pay off that debt with your minimum payment plus your DEA Factor.

Because this is a complex mathematical formula, don't expect to manually calculate each debt individually on this sheet. You must write out the plan with your number one target filled out so you know your focus and the general time frame for termination. I recommend that you copy or tear this page out of the book and put it in your day planner, on your refrigerator, or on your bathroom mirror so you see it every day as a constant reminder of what you want to accomplish.

Table 5.2 shows a sample of a final plan. Using this plan instead of making minimum monthly payments, our fictitious couple will save 1,762 time payments and $18,918 in interest. They will accomplish this by simply adding some extra money to their minimum monthly payments and getting out of the mind-set of keeping payments low. Wouldn't an extra $18,918 come in handy in your future?

TABLE 5.2 MATT AND KATE BOWMAN'S GET OUT OF DEBT PLAN — SAMPLE

My Name: _Matt & Kate Bowman_   **Minimum Payment:** _$647_

Total Debts Owed: _$24,710_   **DEA Factor:** _$278_

Gross Monthly Income: _$6,166_   **Total Amount:** _($925)_

Resolve: Why must I get out of debt now? How will this impact my family and me? _If we keep spending like this, we will wind up broke at age 60, having to work to pay our bills at jobs we hate. We want to be able to help our children get a head start in life and a good education._

Creditor	Balance Owed	Minimum Payment	APR %	DEA Factor	Time Pmts. (in months)
#1 Department store	$1,000	$20	18%	$278	4
#2 Credit card #1	$1,000	$30	12%		
#3 Furniture store	$1,500	$30	16%		
#4 Credit union	$1,500	$30	15%		
#5 Personal loan	$3,000	$60	17%		
#6 Credit card #2	$2,500	$50	17%		
#7 Credit card #3	$2,500	$50	14%		
#8 Auto payment	$12,710	$387	6%		
Totals:	$24,710	$647	------		

TABLE 5.3 MY CREDiT PLAN FOR TOTAL DEBT ELIMINATION

My Name:_____

Total Debts Owed: $_____

Gross Monthly Income: $_____

Minimum Payment: $_____

DEA Factor: $_____

Total Amount: $_____

Resolve: Why must I get out of debt now? How will this impact my family and me?

_____

_____

_____

Creditor	Balance Owed	Minimum Payment	APR %	DEA Factor	Time Pmts. (in months)
#1	$	$	%	$	
#2	$	$	%		
#3	$	$	%		
#4	$	$	%		
#5	$	$	%		
#6	$	$	%		
#7	$	$	%		
#8	$	$	%		
#9	$	$	%		
#10	$	$	%		
Totals:	$	$	------		

"This is my plan for total debt freedom, and I commit from this day forth to do whatever it takes to make this goal a reality. Debt freedom is within me and I will make it happen."

THE TWO ACCELERATORS

Two tools can help you accelerate your plan. If they seem right for you and your circumstances, they will take you more than the promised five minutes but they can help you get out of debt much more quickly and save you more money.

Accelerator #1: Communicate

It is very important to remain in communication with any creditors you have, especially if your payments are past due or you expect future problems. Avoiding creditors can do great damage to your relationship with them and ultimately to your credit file and credit score. As a collector, I always gave greater latitude to the people who kept their promises and stayed in touch with me, whether they paid or not.

In addition, it is not widely known but you can, in many cases, negotiate with lenders to lower your interest rate or sometimes defer interest altogether. If lenders think their account with you is at serious risk they will, in many cases, work with you to help keep the account from getting too far behind.

Years ago I had a business credit card and I never paid attention to the interest rate. When I discovered it was at 19% APR, I promptly picked up the phone and called my bank. In five minutes I had an APR of 14%. Believe it or not, you can negotiate the rate of your loan or credit card, especially if you're in good standing and they're in jeopardy of losing you to another bank with a lower APR.

Accelerator #2: Consolidate

An important thing to remember about this tool is that *consolidation is not elimination.* Many people become confused by this sometimes helpful option. It is only beneficial if you truly resolve to get out of debt and stop overspending by interrupting your current (or past) spending habits. Many people get hypnotized into believing they're saving money with their consolidation plan, when in fact they've lowered their monthly obligation while raising the overall cost significantly, especially when they consolidate via real estate refinance. Think about it. Let's say you have a car loan with two years left to pay. You wrap it into a real estate refinance and that balance is now amortized over 30 years. Of course the payment will go down, but are you really saving anything? The answer is a resounding NO! Again, it's the low monthly payment syndrome. If you can consolidate with lower APRs or even under a real estate refinance, you could save thousands of dollars, but the key again is *how you repay* the debt.

A FINAL NOTE ABOUT DEBT AND YOUR NEWLY CREATED PLAN

Now that your plan is created, I'd like to see you *automate* it as much as possible and then forget about it. That's right, forget about it! Remember, your ultimate goal is not to be debt free, but rather to be *financially independent.* Getting out of debt is just a part of the journey, staying out of debt is another part, but building lasting independence or financial freedom (whatever you want to call it) will inspire you. Put your plan to work, automate it as much as possible, and get it done while focusing on what you ultimately want. Your focus and goal are to stay out of debt by defining and setting a plan in place to create financial independence, a plan that puts you in the position of working because you want to, not because you have to pay your bills.

Most banks and lending institutions send coupons or flyers with their monthly statements, inviting you to participate in an automated clearing house (ACH) or electronic funds transfer (EFT). With these methods, an agreed-upon amount of money is automatically deducted from your checking or savings account on an agreed-upon date. Take advantage of this option as much as possible. If you need to, call your institution to get information on this service. Look out for unnecessary or unreasonable fees.

As you flip the page to the next chapter, focus on what you just created for yourself: a plan that will absolutely create freedom from the burden of debt forever. Let this part of the book go for now. You can always come back and reread this section when you feel you need a reminder or want to rewrite your plan as things change (income, expenses, etc).

Remember the law of attraction that I mentioned earlier? As a reminder, it means that *whatever you focus on, you will get more of or attract into your life.* With this in mind you don't want your central focus to be debt. You want it to be freedom, security, independence, prosperity, wealth, abundance, or whatever else you want for yourself. Think of debt now as your rearview mirror on the road to financial independence. The rearview mirror is important; you need it as a reminder of where you've been and what you're leaving behind and to make sure that no obstacles or interferences creep up behind you. But you wouldn't want to drive your entire trip looking through this part of your financial picture, would you? Of course not! You want to use the windshield, which represents your financial vision, purpose, and long- and short-term goals. This is where the beauty is—the road and the journey in front of you—and this is where your focus needs to be 99% of the time. It's okay to peek in the rearview mirror to make any needed adjustments, but make sure you get back to your windshield right away, as this is where the magic of your financial journey will appear. (That's what we'll create together in the final part of this book.) Of course, you'll need to check in when you eliminate your

number one target or if you have any changes in your income, expenses, or debt burden (which I'm hoping will only go down for you).

The final chapter of part 1 deals with credit. Not the CREDiT Method you just learned but the actual service and privilege available to you called credit and your own personal credit file and credit score. It's important to understand this part of your financial picture and use it to your full and maximum advantage, so let's get started.

*There is no passion to be found in playing small—
in settling for a life that is less than what you are
capable of living.*

~ Nelson Mandela

CHAPTER SIX

Understanding and Utilizing Your Credit Score

In 1977, when I was 14 years old, my mom and dad separated and ultimately divorced. Soon after the divorce, my father unfortunately began to spiral downward, both emotionally and financially. Unbeknownst to me, using my social security number, he put some utility bills in my name and then skipped out on them, leaving the unpaid bills to go ultimately to collection agencies. You can imagine what happened when I applied for my first credit purchase at 20 years old. Not only did I have no credit, I had *bad credit.* Luckily for me, the salesman at the motorcycle dealership, where my sister and I had ventured to buy a motorcycle together, had taken a liking to us. He explained the credit system and told me that I had the right to dispute the outstanding balances in my name and my credit rating. He gave me the address of TRW (now Experian) so I could write to them directly, tell my side of the story, and have those negative accounts removed from my personal credit file. Totally humiliated, I did exactly that.

Through the pain and frustration of that experience, I learned to value my credit score and since then have always taken great pride in protecting my credit rating. It's sad that in America few people know or even seem to care what their credit score is. According to Fair Isaac, the company responsible for creating the popular FICO score, nearly half of all Americans have a poor credit score (a score of 550 or less). The following pages

include a brief overview of this piece of your financial puzzle and why it's so critical to you. You'll discover some simple ideas and a few resources to get you going in the right direction if this is an area you need to focus on. You'll also learn how to evaluate your credit score and examine some simple steps to help you improve it. If you already have a score of at least 700 or higher, you may skip this step.

THE IMPORTANCE OF HAVING A STRONG CREDIT SCORE

Most lenders consider a score of 700 or higher a sign of great financial health. Later in this chapter, I'll share my grading scale for credit scores, and you'll learn how to grade your score on a scale from A to F. A strong credit score (which I define as nothing less than a grade of A) provides the following main benefits:

- It can make the difference in getting approved for borrowing and it can speed up the process (higher scores can mean faster borrowing).

- It can get you lower interest rates on the money you borrow, which can ultimately save you a lot of money.

- It can make the difference in being approved to rent a home or apartment.

- It opens the possibility for lower insurance premiums.

- It can lower deposit amounts on utilities.

- Knowing you have handled this part of your financial success can increase your pride and put the law of attraction to work in your favor.

Obviously the downside of a low score would simply be the opposite of the above list.

A CRASH COURSE IN CREDIT SCORING: WHO IS FAIR ISAAC, ANYWAY?

The Fair Isaac Corporation is an analytical data organization founded in 1956. They created the FICO (**F**air **I**saac **Co**rporation) score as a tool to give lenders a fast, objective measurement of your personal credit risk. Fair Isaac considers themselves the X-ray for the lending industry and reports that 90% of the largest U.S. banks use the FICO scoring system as a measuring tool. Recently some credit bureaus have attempted to create their own scoring system, but FICO has remained the brand and standard in the industry.

FICO uses a scoring range of 300–850. Like other analytical tools, the FICO score is a complicated formula that takes into account many variables within your own personal scenario. It's not as important to get caught up in *how* they come up with the figures as it is to know *what* yours is and how to raise it if you have a C rating or below (where you really start to feel the negative financial impact of a low score).

Your FICO score takes five elements into account:

- **Payment history:** What's your track record?
- **Amount owed:** How much is too much?
- **Length of credit history:** How established is yours?
- **New credit:** Are you taking on new debt?
- **Types of credit in use:** Is it a healthy mix?

In addition to your actual score, your lender receives a list referred to as "score reasons." These reasons can sometimes be more important than the score itself in regard to lenders making a decision. When you receive your credit report, you can also request the legend of reason codes. Knowing the reasons can help you identify possible errors on your report and identify what you can do to raise your score.

Much like a wound or an injury, your credit score can decline (get injured) much faster than it can be raised (heal or recover). You can, however, take actions to make a measurable difference in your score *over time*. It's important to avoid going for the quick fix, like hiring someone else or paying a service to clean up your score, but rather to methodically do the things that will increase your score over time. The top things you can do to increase your score, in order of importance, are:

1. Pay your bills on time.

2. Settle any collection or past due accounts.

3. Keep your owed balances down.

4. Keep older accounts open; don't just close them for convenience.

5. Don't open new accounts often.

Every person's scenario is different, so the impact of the positive actions you take will be different from that of someone else.

If you already know your score, write it in the following table so you can grade yourself. If you don't know your score, I want to challenge you

TABLE 6.1 FICO: WHAT'S YOUR SCORE?

My FICO Score	My Score
You can get a free copy of your credit report at https://www.annualcreditreport.com/cra/index.jsp	
However, if you want your FICO credit score it will cost approximately $15.95 from Equifax at http://www.equifax.com	**Evaluation Scale** 700–850 = A 620–699 = B
You can also get your FICO score from the Experian Web site at http://www.freecreditreport.com (3 reports and 3 scores for approximately $40)	600–619 = C 500–599 = D 300–499 = F

right now to obtain it by going online (see instructions below) or writing to your credit bureau (the addresses are listed at the end of this chapter).

The preceding evaluation scale is my own scoring system, created with the help of some associates who have a combined 50 years working in the lending industry. The breaking points are based on where the lenders have hits (decreases) on your lending power based on your personal score. For example, if you have a score lower than 620, you would have to go to sub-prime lenders that have higher rates, so that's a critical cutoff point on the scale.

Sometimes little things can make a big difference in your score and ultimately the price you pay. A few years ago, I attempted to refinance my mortgage at a lower interest rate. My mortgage broker said I had a blemish on my credit report (a nice way to say that a negative account had shown up). The negative mark resulted from a $200 medical bill that had gone to a collection agency. Years before, I had flatly refused to pay a doctor for what I felt was poor and misleading medical advice. I promised myself that I would not pay the bill as a matter of principle and I became very stubborn over the issue. When it came time to refinance my home, my broker was going to have to raise my interest rate by one-quarter of one percent (.25%) because of the impact on my credit score. I did the math on the total cost difference over the life of my mortgage and the amount was significant. It was a tough decision but wanting to be smart with my money I settled the collection account to raise my credit score and get the lower interest rate. That simple action meant a savings of tens of thousands of dollars on my new mortgage. Of course I have a plan to accelerate my mortgage anyway but I figured why not save any additional money while I can.

Don't let your pride or negative past experiences get in the way of keeping an outstanding credit score. Most important, don't let fear stop you from taking action on past due accounts. I believe that people can

become afraid to communicate with collection agencies or lenders because of embarrassment or humiliation over past experiences. Let it go and call them to make things right.

WHO ARE THE PLAYERS IN CREDIT REPORTING?

Credit reporting first appeared more than 100 years ago when individuals went from merchant to merchant in a town or city, taking notes about how customers repaid their debts. The merchants could then ask for credit references based on the notes kept in local credit bureau files. Eventually, credit reporting expanded, automated, and consolidated into three regional credit-reporting companies:

- **Experian** (formerly TRW) evolved in the west and is now based in Costa Mesa, California.

- **TransUnion**, based in Chicago, grew in the central United States.

- **Equifax**, in Atlanta, dominated the south and east.

With computer and technology advances that virtually eliminated geographic limitations, these organizations now compete globally. It's important to note that they can all report your FICO score differently, but variances are typically minimal unless there is a significant error on one report versus another.

These organizations offer many services that can be helpful to you; however, you need to look carefully at whether the service or product is a wise use of your money. Like many organizations these days, they have subscription-based services where you can be informed about your credit report 24/7. I don't think I'm sold on the necessity of this service unless you've been a recent victim of credit fraud or identity theft, but you should evaluate this for yourself.

A Few Myths about Credit Reports and Scores

Myth #1: Checking your own credit report will hurt your score.

Fact: Personal inquiries, also known as soft inquiries, are not included in your credit report and therefore are not part of your credit score calculation. Checking your own report will not lower your score.

Myth #2: Your score is the only thing that matters to a creditor.

Fact: When determining whether to extend credit, grantors may consider a number of other factors, such as your income, assets, length at current residency, and employment history, in addition to your credit score. The criteria may also differ from creditor to creditor.

Myth #3: Your credit score never changes.

Fact: Your credit score is a dynamic number based on the contents of your credit report and generated the moment it is requested. Since your credit report changes constantly, so will your credit score.

What's an Insurance Score?

Insurance companies believe there is a correlation between credit history and the likelihood of someone filing a claim. Almost 90% of auto insurance companies and an increasing number of home insurers use credit information to determine your premiums. The insurance industry has also added a scoring system based on your credit score to determine your overall insurance costs and whether they will insure you at all. The higher your credit score, the higher the probability that you will receive

lower premiums. Conversely, the lower your credit score, the higher your insurance costs can be.

If you could keep your insurance premiums lower with good credit habits, wouldn't you want to do so? Good credit habits and lower insurance premiums can only help you accelerate your plan for financial independence.

A Client Takes Action to Change Her Circumstances

I'll end this chapter with a short story about one of my coaching clients who decided to raise her credit score in 2002, when it reached a low of 525 (a solid D on my rating scale). I'm including her story as a reference for you, affirming that it can be done; it just takes focus, communication, time, and patience.

After some one-on-one coaching, Marshonda took on the project of increasing her credit score to avail her of the many benefits described in this chapter. Like me, she was a victim of her family's abuse of her personal credit file: they put utility bills in her name and neglected to pay them. In Pittsburgh, Pennsylvania, where Marshonda grew up, a winter gas and electric bill can be several hundred dollars in a month and her family saw this as the only option to keep their home warm. When she became aware of this, not understanding the many benefits borrowing can create, she took actions (or lack thereof) that made her credit score even worse over time. This coupled with living off credit cards while she attended college created a debt nightmare.

At one point Marshonda owed more than $14,000 in bad credit, which is usually credit that the lender has written off (and in most cases given up trying to collect). She hired a third-party company to help her clean things up but they over-promised and under-delivered on their results and she wound up doing most of the work herself. This work included contacting every past-due account and letting each creditor know of her intent to repay the balance. In some cases she negotiated a zero balance with a one-time cash payment of 75 cents on the dollar and sometimes even less. Other actions she took involved connecting directly with the credit bureaus to change or correct misinformation, since some of her accounts were showing up twice (once with the original lender and again with the collection agency). She took other actions—again, *over time*— to get some of her balances below 50% of the credit limit on the account (this has a significant impact on the score).

I sincerely hope that learning a little bit about Marshonda's journey may inspire you to pick up the phone or pull out a pen and paper and begin your own journey if you need to do so but have been putting it off. *Marshonda's score in 2006 was 711,* an A on my scale. Raising her score had a tremendous impact not only on her ability to borrow (she was denied a store credit card at one point) but also on the interest rate she pays, her cash flow (important because she has become a real estate investor), and even the way she walks and talks as a leader and a woman with power.

Now that you have your fail-safe get-out-of-debt plan and you've had a crash course in credit scores, let's get into the more exciting part of the program, which is to craft this next level of success for you. The next few chapters are all about *staying out of debt forever* and defining what you need to create the lifestyle you truly want, desire, and deserve.

HOW TO CONTACT THE THREE MAJOR CREDIT BUREAUS

TransUnion
P.O. Box 6790
Fullerton, CA 92834
Web: http://www.transunion.com/
Free annual credit report: (877) 322-8228

Experian
Web: http://www.experian.com/
By phone: (888) 397 3742

Equifax Credit Information Services, Inc.
P.O. Box 740241
Atlanta, GA 30374
Web: http://www.equifax.com/home/
Order credit report by phone: (800) 685-1111

PART TWO

Stay Out of Debt Forever

If we don't believe something is possible, we will find all sorts of obstacles to get in our way.

~ Louise Hay

CHAPTER SEVEN

Wealth Traits: Building Your Foundation for Success

For nearly all of us the journey for long-term financial success is just that: *a journey.* Few people get rich quick or sustain that wealth, even though it seems to be the ill-prepared hope of many. This is not a statement of negativity or pessimism but rather a request to consider that your journey is predicated on your preparedness and your ability to take advantage of opportunities along the way. Your success (or lack thereof) will be what you make of it day to day, week to week, month to month, and year to year. My true hope with this book is that you will put a solid, well-thought-out plan in place so that, should you hit the jackpot or win the lottery or inherit a huge sum of money, it will simply be the icing on the cake and not your only game plan for financial independence.

We've all heard the saying, "It's the journey, not the destination, that matters." In any navigation process, you have to *prepare your mind* for the journey ahead, not only to get through the process but also to help you enjoy the process while you prosper. To increase your chances of long-term, sustainable wealth, there are many aspects of your psychology or mind-set that you can work to improve. I call these wealth traits. In school, most of us were educated about history, math, language, and other traditional subjects but *we were not formally taught how to create long-term sustainable wealth.* When we were old enough for the lending and credit

card companies to get their hands on us (which appears to be earlier and earlier), we were trained to focus on two questions:

- Do I want this? (Of course the answer is YES.)
- Can I afford the low monthly payment?

If there's one thing I want you get from this book, it's the motivation to create more powerful and resourceful questions that will lead you to a more powerful financial destiny. *Better quality questions will lead to a better quality of life.* This lesson and skill are among the most important I've learned in my life. This chapter will help you explore facets of your psychology and mind-set that enable you to more powerfully and elegantly achieve your financial dreams and goals while living a happier, healthier, and wealthier life. I've listed 12 traits of successful people that I believe, once recognized and embraced, will have a profound impact on where you wind up financially. Ten are things you do, and two are things you avoid. With each wealth trait, I've also included some questions for you to consider. Again, you'll benefit most from this exercise by answering each question as accurately and honestly as you can.

WEALTH TRAIT #1:
Successful People Have Powerful Belief Systems That Support Their Success

This chapter begins with a quote about belief systems from world-renowned author and metaphysical lecturer Louise Hay: "If we don't believe something is possible, we will find all sorts of obstacles to get in our way." I can't think of a more elegant way to put it. Beliefs give us the power to manifest or tear apart whatever we want in our lives. Automotive pioneer Henry Ford said, "Whether you believe you can or you can't, you're right." These are powerful and profound words from a man who changed the way we lived simply by turning his ideas into something tangible: the mass-produced automobile. So, what is a belief? The Oxford American Dictionary defines it as "the feeling that something is real or true." If you stop to think about it, a belief is an *idea* that manifests itself into emotion that carries with it a relative amount of *certainty.* The more certain you feel, the stronger the belief within you.

The greatest challenge we face regarding our beliefs is to evaluate not whether they are right or wrong, good or bad, stupid or smart, but whether they support us in achieving what we want for our lives. I don't know if I could give you more potent advice than to evaluate what you believe about money, finances, and debt. I can give you all the tools and resources in the world for dealing with these issues, but if your beliefs don't support the same outcome, the tools will do you no good. For example, if I give you the greatest, most proven strategy for rapid debt elimination but you believe that debt isn't that bad, or even worse, that debt is good, or that low monthly payments allow you to afford things more easily, you'll continue to find ways to get back into debt. On the opposite side, if people believe that paying cash for consumer purchases allows them to save more, they are much more likely to save more.

Take a moment right now to evaluate one or more beliefs you have about money that may not be supporting you or may be holding you back from achieving more for yourself or your family.

1. **Write down a negative belief you have about money, wealth, finances, or debt (such as "Wealthy people are greedy" or "I don't deserve to have money"):**

   _____

2. **Write down the source of this belief (such as your father or mother, a relative, a book, or an experience you had):**

   _____

96

3. Looking back, did this belief come from a source you now respect in terms of financial success and what you want for yourself today?

       Yes   No   (circle one)

4. Write down all the reasons this belief no longer supports you and what you want for your life:

_____

_____

_____

_____

5. Write down a *new belief* (maybe the opposite of the old one) that better supports who you are today and what you want for yourself and your family:

_____

6. Write why you can and will believe this now. What references do you have to support this belief? Why does this new belief support you and what you want?

_____

_____

_____

_____

In doing this exercise you may have explored a belief to which you had a relative amount of certainty attached. Depending on the amount of certainty, you may have completely shifted to a new belief that more fully supports who you are and what you want today. If you chose a belief that you have very strong certainty about, known as a *conviction,* you may need something a little more earthshaking than an exercise like this. If you have a very strong belief within you that really limits your potential, I suggest you consider attending a seminar or event, or possibly getting a coach to help you break this belief. If you need help with this, please contact me directly through my Web site and I'll see what I can do to assist you.

As I stated earlier, nothing is more powerful to build or destroy than a belief. Although you can easily shift a belief, doing so typically requires you to be in a position where you must make the shift. That usually occurs when you have a tremendous amount of pain associated with not changing the belief and you start to see the benefits of making the change. It is also important to mention that your beliefs should serve the greater good. I mention the greater good because life is not just about benefiting yourself while negatively impacting others; rather, it is about *serving others while attaining all that you want.*

WEALTH TRAIT #2:
Successful People Consistently Spend Less Than They Earn

At a fundamental level there are only two things you can do with your money: you can save it or you can spend it on the things you want and need. Sometimes we fool ourselves into thinking we need something we really just want. However, successful people know that *the number one key to financial success is to consistently spend less than you earn and save the difference.* Once again, the standard we use is a minimum of 10%.

Assuming that you are not saving as much as you could or would like to, let me ask you a question. If you lost 10% of your income right now,

would you figure out a way to get by? Of course you would. You'd find something to cut or adjust because you'd have no other choice. This is exactly the mind-set and standard of people who build long-term wealth: they figure out a way to get by and succeed while setting 10% of their earnings aside.

When I personally coach people they usually start out with the story, "I can't afford to save right now." They approach the game with the psychology that says, "Someday when I make more money or pay off this credit card, then I'll save." I know you don't want to hear this but *someday will never come* because as you make more money you'll create new ways to spend it. You may have heard the saying, "The road called someday leads to a town called nowhere."

If you decide today that you'll always save X% of your gross earnings, no matter what, you'll begin to see a huge shift in your ability to create and manifest your goals. I've mentioned *The Richest Man in Babylon* throughout this book, where author George Clason has set the standard for saving a minimum of 10%. His book, often referred to as the bible of personal finances, tells us that following this principle will shift your psychology to that of a successful money manager and a person of personal wealth.

Another golden nugget I pulled from Clason's book is "Gold avoids those unwise in its use." It's hard to say this without sounding too esoteric, but I do believe there is a financial universe of energy surrounding money and that Clason's statement is completely true. If you're not wise with your money, it will go to someone who is. I'm sure you've heard the statement, "The rich get richer." Rich people have proven to this universe of energy that they are worthy of that gold (money) and that they will take care of it (save, invest, protect, and monitor).

If there's one thing I've learned over the years it's that *if you ignore your money, it will go away.* You have to create a plan for measuring and monitoring your monthly income and expenses so you'll know where you are from month to month. The same is true with health, relationships, happiness, and nearly every other area of life. You can't manage what you don't measure. Make saving a must, by spending less than you earn, and you'll see your financial universe open up to unlimited possibilities. We'll talk more about this and create a detailed savings plan in part 3 of this book.

WEALTH TRAIT #3:
Successful People Use Words That Create Success

The Bible says, "That which we speak we become." When it comes to finances, the words we use to describe who we are, what we want, or what holds us back can have a huge impact, positive or negative. Like beliefs, words can bring us up or tear us down. I've had a lot of lessons in my lifetime and I've found this to be true: The words you use to describe your financial condition will *become* your financial condition.

You have to choose your words wisely. Are you barely getting by or are you a millionaire in the making? Are you making ends meet or are you kicking butt and taking names? I pulled a great nugget about getting out of debt from a book that was otherwise lacking in powerful ideas. The author talked about visualizing what you want and then speaking about it. In that moment I decided to start saying, "I will pay off my home mortgage in seven years." I didn't have a plan at the time but I started saying it to friends, family, associates, and myself, and I still say it today. Less than two years into our mortgage, my wife and I had reduced it by over 30%. I have since created a more specific plan to eliminate the mortgage, but I truly believe that simply repeating that sentence created a whole new focus and momentum in that direction.

If you don't say anything about your debt plan then you will most likely fall victim to the amortization schedules put before you. Those plans will squash your chances of getting out of debt because *loan companies and*

banks want to keep you in debt as long as possible and for as much profit as possible. Their mantra is "Low monthly payments." Mine is "I pay cash for everything." Choose your words wisely as you create your plan.

Over the years, I've collected some of the phrases I've heard when asking people how they were doing financially. The following are words and phrases commonly used by people to describe their financial situation, whether consciously or unconsciously (on automatic pilot). Do any of these sound familiar to you?

Positive	**Not So Positive, or Negative**
Rich	Getting by
Billionaire	Hangin' in there
Striking it rich	Big hat, no cattle
Decca-millionaire	Barely making it
Millionaire	Holding it together
Affluent	Having an out-of-money experience
Prosperous	Living paycheck to paycheck
Set for life	So broke I can't pay attention
Well-to-do	Dirt poor
Wealthy	Piss poor
Abundant	Busted broke
Free	Flat broke
Independent	In the hole
Vital	In the toilet
Millionaire in training	Robbing Peter to pay Paul
Assured	Penniless
Secure	Making ends meet
Protected	Having the disease "fundsarelow"

Take an honest moment right now and write down your canned response when having a conversation about money and someone asks you "How's it going?"

_____

_____

_____

_____

Now write down the way you will answer this question from now on (obviously stated in a much more powerful and positive manner):

_____

_____

_____

_____

Take a few moments to repeat your new answer over and over again until it is imprinted on your mind. If you're sitting down, stand up and put body gestures into it. I know this sounds silly but engaging your body and mind simultaneously can help you anchor your thoughts into your subconscious. Remember, you are what you say so speak powerfully, positively, and with a vision of how you want things to be.

WEALTH TRAIT #4:
Successful People Consistently Ask Quality Questions That Lead to Success

In his runaway best seller *Awaken the Giant Within*, Tony Robbins devoted an entire chapter to the importance of asking quality questions. I highly recommend his book because it contains powerful tools and ideas for creating success in your life and your finances. Robbins says that "all change starts with a question and all progress starts with an even better question." He also adds, "If you want to have a better quality of life, ask a better question."

The 5-Minute Debt Solution evolved from the questions I asked myself about how I could help as many people as possible get out of debt as fast and as easily as possible while enjoying the process. Remember, banks and financial and marketing institutions will ask you questions in an effort to control the questions you ask yourself. Consider this scenario: They provide you with a low monthly payment option and then ask, "Can you afford this?" I would venture to guess that 99.9% of the time the answer to this question is yes because they get their potential customers to focus on a different piece of the puzzle—whether they can afford the low monthly payment. What if *you* started asking the following questions before you made a purchase?

- Do I really want to pay $2,100 for an item that costs only $1,500?

- Did I consider the *cost of borrowing* and how it will affect my overall financial plan?

- Did I consider how much I can save if I save the money first, then come back next year and pay cash?

- Do I need this item or is it something I want and can really do without?

- Would the money I'd be paying in interest be better off invested in a stock or mutual fund?

- Would I be better off buying stock in the company than buying the product itself?

- Where is this money coming from? Have I earned it or do I still have to work for it?

- Should I consider buying this when it's less popular and therefore less expensive?

Before purchasing something, wealthy people ask themselves these types of questions to help them focus on the *total cost* or the *consequences* of their actions. In the 1970s Peter Lynch, one of the greatest money managers and investors of our era, asked a better question when his kids took him shopping at a Gap store. When he got there, he saw that the parking lot was full and the cash register lines were out the door. As consumers pulled items off the shelves and asked themselves, "Do I look good in this?" Lynch asked a very different question: "I wonder if this is a public company?" After careful evaluation, he decided to purchase stock in the company. Since he was a money manager at the time, that purchase made him and many others very wealthy.

The 5-Minute Debt Solution is predicated on three questions:

1. How can I get out of debt as fast as possible and for as little interest expense as possible?

2. How can I stay out of debt forever?

3. How can I build my financial independence?

Before you part with your hard-earned money, I challenge you to ask better questions, such as: How will this purchase affect my goals? Did I plan for this purchase or am I acting on impulse? How hard did I have to

work for the money I'm about to spend? If you ask better questions about your personal finances, you'll get much better results in the days, weeks, and years to come.

WEALTH TRAIT #5:
Successful People Have Values in Alignment with Financial Success

What you value—the emotional states of mind you identify as most important to feel—plays a significant role in how much success you achieve in the financial game. If you value security, you'll play the game very differently than someone who values adventure. Your values are shaped to a large degree by the same forces that created the beliefs you hold important.

In my seminars I see that people often value what they feel they lacked as children. They consequently make those things so important in their minds that they govern many of their adult decisions. For instance, if you grew up with a parent or mentor who didn't save a penny and never knew where the money for the next meal was coming from, you may value financial security or independence more than people who grew up wealthy and got everything they wanted. The same is true of the opposite side of the scale. You've probably heard many stories of people who grew up dirt poor and vowed that they would no longer experience the emotions they had as children, nor would their families.

Two great questions you may want to ask yourself are: What's most important to me regarding finances? and What did my parents or family value as I grew up and how has that impacted me? In this process you want to determine whether you're chasing an emotion you may have lacked as a child or placing value on something you really want for your future. Values play an important role in how you make financial decisions. They are neither wrong nor right, as long as they ultimately give you what you're *really* after.

WEALTH TRAIT #6:
Successful People Look at Problems in a Unique Way

Let me start this one off by asking you a question. Which problem would you rather have:

    A. You can't make your $400 rent payment

    B. You can't make your $4,000 mortgage payment

I sincerely hope you picked answer B. If you didn't, you may want to consider a change in your philosophy regarding financial problems.

Jim Rohn, a leading motivational speaker, author, and another mentor of mine, explained the principle behind this wealth trait when he said, "Don't wish your problems were easier, wish you were better." If you wish for easier problems, that's exactly what you'll get. However, it's the difficult, more challenging problems that make you grow. I can think of few worse things than having the same problem for 10 years. That would be a sign that you're not growing, becoming more, or being resourceful as a human being to better your circumstances.

A lot of people have plenty of money but are miserable inside. You don't want to be one of them. People like Elvis Presley, Chris Farley, John Belushi, and Anna Nicole Smith had plenty of money and opportunities but were miserable and unhappy. They could not deal with their problems so their lives ended tragically. These incredible people were rich in their bank accounts but they weren't wealthy because they didn't have the internal resources or fortitude to solve their problems.

When you're wealthy emotionally, spiritually, and financially, no problem is insurmountable. Think about a really big problem you had 10 or 15 years ago. When you think about that problem now, how does it make you feel? Do you feel like you could handle it easily now? Does the thought of dealing with something like that seem insignificant now?

Do you have the emotional muscle to handle something of this level should it arise again? If the answer is yes, it's because you've grown and become more.

If you're going to play the financial game, you *will* have problems. This is guaranteed. The goal of the game is not to be problem free but to have problems that challenge you to become more and move on from them.

WEALTH TRAIT #7:
Successful People Treat Their Personal Finances Like a Business

Do you spend your money like a consumer or like a profitable business? If your personal finances were a business, would your friends and associates want to invest in it? Most important, do you have more money saved and invested at the end of the year than you had at the beginning? I challenge you to think about the fact that *you are in business,* the business of building financial independence for yourself and your family. If you are also an entrepreneur and own your own company, then you have at least two businesses.

If you stopped working today, how long could you continue to pay for your monthly and yearly obligations without returning to work? Statistics show that the average American family is 2.5 paychecks from bankruptcy. Remember, the ultimate goal is to work because you're fulfilled by what you do instead of working simply to pay your bills. The popular (and derogatory) saying "I owe, I owe, it's off to work I go" is not inspiring. From now on, I want you to think of your money or portfolio as a widget factory. Your factory is made up of the savings and investments assets that bring you income. Obviously, the bigger the factory, the more income it will produce. Your factory's productivity must increase until its income can meet or surpass the income you make by going to work.

In my live and online seminars I ask people to come up with a name for their factory, and I'm going to ask you to do the same thing right now. Giving your finances a name will promote a feeling of personal pride that will cause you to treat them like a real entity instead of a mere bank or brokerage account and keep you more focused on your company's success. Naming your factory, portfolio, or business is particularly beneficial because words strongly influence how you feel and therefore your actions. When my wife and I did this exercise several years ago, it changed how we felt about our finances. The name of our company is Millions in Motion, and although we don't yet have the millions we ultimately want, the name conjures up a vision that makes us take the actions to make our savings and investments grow with each passing year.

If you were going to name your business right now, what would it be? Take a moment to create a name for your factory. Think of a name that feels creative, playful, fun, and exciting, so that you will check in regularly and ask the question, *How's business*? Write that name in the space below:

> **The name of my/our company is:**
>
> _____
>
> **And I am/we are in the business of building financial independence.**

Here are some sample business names created by past graduates of my coaching program:

- Me Inc.
- Money Machine, Inc.

- Freedom Corporation

- Dollars R Us

- Mano-E-Mano (hand in hand)

- P.A.W. Inc. (Perpetual Accumulator of Wealth)

- The Dollar Factory

- The Road to San Carlos

If you're married or have a partner, involve him/her in this exercise. Come up with a name that excites you both and gets you working together. My wife and I regularly schedule quarterly and annual company meetings on Saturday mornings. Before, it sometimes seemed as if she wasn't particularly interested in our finances, but now she reminds me, "We're having our quarterly meeting for Millions in Motion this weekend, aren't we?"

You don't have to come up with the perfect name right this minute. My wife and I found that naming our company was a process but we finally came up with the right name and it has stuck with us for many years. At least brainstorm a few names right now. Remember, the key is to make the name something playful and fun, as well as one that invites a powerful emotional response. I currently use a leading brand of personal finance software as one of the tools to manage my finances, and I reinforce the emotional effect by putting our company name on all the reports and graphs it generates. Some of my clients have even gone so far as to draw up logos and designs to make their company name more visual and compelling. There aren't many rules here. Just do whatever will keep you focused, excited, and motivated to improve this area of your life and feel a sense of pride for what you're building.

WEALTH TRAIT #8:
Successful People Know How to Manage Urgency and Scarcity

If you're in debt, it's simply because you've spent more than you earned and borrowed the difference. That's it! Overspending is usually a response to a sense of urgency, and people who stay out of debt know how to manage this powerful force. When you're vulnerable, you can end up fighting a psychological battle against the intelligent and powerful organizations that want you to believe that having their products and services is not only important, but it's *urgent*. Their messages consistently say, "You'd better do it *now* or your chance will be gone forever!" Please realize that these organizations use urgency and scarcity as subconscious tools. They know that if you don't do it now, you probably won't do it at all.

These implied commands are tied to nearly every marketing message you see or hear. Have you ever seen a TV infomercial or commercial that said, "Take down our number and call us in the next few days or when you get a chance, and we'll be here to help you?" Hardly. It's always about NOW. *Hurry, call now, only a few hours left, limited seating, the sale ends Sunday, do it now and you'll receive this free gift.*

Successful people remind themselves that this is just a technique used by advertisers to put you into a hypnotic trance and get you to pick up the phone or drive to your local mattress store. Let me ask you a question: When was the last time Sears *didn't* have a sale? Maybe 1975? I'm on their e-mail list and, without exaggeration, I can honestly say I get sales announcements from them just about every week. Don't get me wrong— I love Sears and I think their marketing strategy is brilliant. But it's important to recognize marketing strategies when you see them and not get caught up in the false urgency they can project.

If you can prevent scarcity and urgency from causing you to make decisions you may later regret, you will have eliminated two obstacles

that stand in the way of your progress toward your goals. It's also important to mention that these two forces have their time and place and can be important in your life. People who achieve long-term financial success make their *own goals* urgent. You, too, must create a sense of urgency within yourself to build and sustain the momentum required to reach your financial goals. For example, you could shift your urgency for purchasing that new big-screen HDTV to putting the same amount of money into an investment that will grow over time.

WEALTH TRAIT #9:
Successful People Understand the Millionaire's Ladder

In assessing their personal finances, people commonly tend to focus on their net worth rather than their critical mass. There's an important distinction between these two definitions of wealth. Net worth is measured by subtracting total liabilities from total assets, while critical mass includes only the cash and investments that generate income or cash flow. Although we've been taught that net worth is the measuring stick, I contend that it's not. Focusing on net worth alone can give you a false impression of your ability to generate an income without working (the very definition of financial independence).

To illustrate the difference, I offer the image of the millionaire's ladder, on which you climb step by step to reach your critical mass at the top.

FIGURE 7.1 THE MILLIONAIRE'S LADDER

$1 Million in Critical Mass

(The amount of money you have invested. Your new standard for wealth.)

$1 Million in Net Worth*

(All assets minus all liabilities)

$1 Million in Assets

*Standard U.S. definition of a millionaire

Relying on net worth alone is not an accurate method for determining your ability to generate cash flow while being independent of work because your net worth includes assets that you may never convert to cash. Your cars, jewelry, home equity, toys, and other collectibles will not help you achieve financial independence unless you decide to "sell the farm" and turn these assets into cash and investments. Then you will have converted to critical mass.

In their mega–best seller *The Millionaire Next Door,* Thomas Stanley and William Danko refer to people who use this method as "under accumulators of wealth" or UAWs. I like to refer to them as posers. They look like they're doing well because they have all the "stuff" but they don't have the financial foundation in place. They're *posing* as the well-to-do.

I propose that critical mass needs to be your central focus because it allows you to create a lifestyle that is independent from work. When you focus on critical mass, you'll see a corresponding shift in your attitude that will create a stronger pull toward financial freedom. You are now focused on generating the possibility for cash flow rather than accumulating things that may not bring income. I'm not saying you shouldn't buy things; just know the consequences of your spending and how it impacts your true objective of creating independence.

Let me give you an example. Assume two people receive $5,000 bonuses and they each decide to buy a watch. Person A purchases a $5,000 Rolex; his net worth has now increased by $5,000 (or less if the watch does not retain its value). Person A's critical mass has not increased at all. Person B buys a $300 watch and puts the remaining $4,700 into an interest-earning money market account. His net worth has increased by $4,700 (assuming the watch does not hold its value). More important, his critical mass has increased by the same amount and it will continue to increase if he reinvests the interest he earns or moves the money to another type of investment that grows over time.

Person B's watch may not go up in value but he doesn't care because that's not his focus. When purchasing the watch, he asked a different question: How will this purchase affect my critical mass? In contrast, Person A believes he is fine because he knows that his Rolex will more than likely hold its value. The major difference is that Person A has no potential for increasing his income unless he sells the watch for a profit, but then he wouldn't know what time it was.

It's important to evaluate the financial decisions you make by asking this critical question: By spending this money, am I increasing my critical mass, building my net worth, or neither? *The Millionaire Next Door* refers to people who consistently ask this question and continue to build their critical mass as perpetual accumulators of wealth, or PAWs. Which would you rather be?

The following tables compare a person's critical mass to net worth.

TABLE 7.1 SAMPLE CRITICAL MASS REPORT

Matt & Kate Bowman's Critical Mass Report
As of 12/31/2007

ASSETS

Cash & Bank Accounts

ABC Bank—Savings	$800

Investments

Portfolio Account	$18,000
Money Market	$1,000
401(k)	$3,500
Total Investment Assets	**$ 23,300**

TABLE 7.2 SAMPLE NET WORTH REPORT

Matt & Kate Bowman's Net Worth Report
As of 12/31/2007

ASSETS

Cash & Bank Accounts

ABC Bank—Primary Checking	$300
ABC Bank—Checking	$500
ABC Bank—Savings	$800

Other Assets

Automobile	$4,000
Household Assets	$10,000
Jewelry & Art	$2,000
Our Home	$195,000
Investments	
Portfolio Account	$18,000
Money Market	$1,000
401(k)	$3,500

Total Assets	**$235,100**

LIABILITIES

Other Liabilities

Mortgage	$150,000
Visa	$5,000
MasterCard	$3,000
Department Store Revolving	$900
Furniture Store	$1,200

Total Liabilities	**<$160,100>**

Overall Total and Net Worth	**$ 75,000**

You'll notice that the equity value of the couple's home is not included in the critical mass statement. Since you'll always have to live somewhere, we don't count home equity (home value minus mortgage amount) unless you sell your home. Even then, you'll more than likely have to buy another home. The equity value of investment property (such as a second home or rental property) would be counted because you can sell that property without affecting where you live.

You do want to think about and check on your net worth, but ultimately it's your critical mass that will generate your future income. The more you focus on growing it, the more likely you are to attain that goal (remember the law of attraction).

When evaluating your net worth, look at all of the assets you own. Remember that you always have the choice to identify personal items of value (art, jewelry, collectibles, luxury items, etc.) that you no longer want or need and convert them to cash. This money can now be applied toward your investments and your critical mass.

WEALTH TRAIT #10:
Successful People Know How to Manage the Law of Familiarity

This principle is particularly meaningful to me because I'm faced with this issue as I write these pages. My wife and I recently purchased a used vehicle that was significantly newer and more luxurious than our previous two cars. This car will be hers and the family car. I drive a relatively nice but older car, a 1995 Lexus GS-300. When I first sat in the Lexus, I thought I had arrived. It was my dream car! In the eight-plus years that I've been driving this car, I've kept it in relatively good condition and there's nothing wrong with it. However, I've become familiar with my car and now I find myself (especially after driving our new car over the weekend) thinking that I need a new car.

When things become overly familiar, they tend to lose their value. This deceptive feeling of familiarity can push you to purchase things you don't really need, trapping and snaring you in all areas of life. Fortunately, there are three things you can do to overcome this negative dynamic and BAN the familiar feeling.

> **B** - Change what you *believe* about the item and make sure your beliefs support what you ultimately want.

> **A** - Focus on what you *appreciate* about the item you have.

> **N** - *Notice* what's great about the item or why you loved it so much in the beginning.

When I find myself feeling like I need a new car, I remind myself of the first day I sat in my current car. I focus on what I *believed, appreciated,* and *noticed* that day and take myself back to that state of mind. This doesn't mean I won't ever buy a new car, but the BAN process removes the sense of urgency that makes me think I need to buy it today. I'm certainly not saying that you should drive an old, broken-down piece of junk, but you have to be careful about telling yourself you need something that you really just want.

Before we go any further, take a moment to think about something you own right now that you'd like to replace. Ask yourself what you could believe, appreciate, and notice that would make you change the way you feel about the item, at least until you have a plan to replace or upgrade it. People who have achieved long-term financial success consistently ask these questions and go through this process. They look at their long-term plans and goals and evaluate how each purchase affects their plan to keep on course. That's true wealth navigation.

WEALTH TRAIT #11:
Successful People Don't Play the Lottery

Many people live their financial lives with something I call the lottery syndrome. Somewhere in the back of their minds they believe they will suddenly become rich one day. Consequently, they don't do the small things day to day and month to month to create sustainable wealth.

Lottery syndrome is an extremely destructive mind-set. If you find yourself thinking this way, it's essential to rid yourself of those thoughts. The best thing you can do is go back to the exercise on beliefs in this chapter and work to uncover any underlying beliefs that are keeping you in this pattern. It's not wise to think that your financial nest egg will magically appear, and getting rich quick simply doesn't work. If you don't have a foundation in place that includes clear goals, an empowering mind-set, and a way to see exactly where you are, no amount of money will solve your problems; it will only make them worse.

I once heard money described as a magnifier because it magnifies what and who you already are. In other words, if a total jerk gets a lot of money, he becomes a bigger jerk. If an incredibly giving and loving person gets more money, she becomes more of a giver. If you have a lot of unsolved problems, gaining money only makes your problems bigger.

I once saw a newscast that was promoting the weekly lottery jackpot. The station held a poll and asked its viewers, "How would you spend $25 million?" Notice the presupposition in this question. The station presupposed that the winner would *spend* all the money because most people probably would.

To avoid lottery syndrome, you must have a plan in place. Then if you hit the jackpot by inheritance, lottery, lawsuit, or some other fortunate circumstance, the money will only accelerate your progress. By adopting

the identity of a wealthy person, you'll already have proven that you're wise enough to handle whatever comes your way.

WEALTH TRAIT #12:
Successful People Don't Let Financial Setbacks Become Financial Ruin

Most people who have accumulated long-term, sustained wealth have also dealt with major problems, setbacks, failures, or losses along the way. Just as they dealt with their problems, they also used their setbacks as *learning experiences* rather than obstacles that kept them from achieving what they wanted. Their vision, purpose, goals, and perhaps most important their *identity,* were bigger than anything that happened to them.

What sets these people apart from those who fall into financial ruin or permanent despair? Those who have mastered this wealth trait have decided it's more important to hold onto what they value most, learn from their experiences, and move on. I didn't say this was easier, I said it was more important. It's much easier to give up or say things like "Why try?" than to rise above whatever challenges you may encounter. The wealthy stay focused and use their negative experiences as a way to learn, grow, and succeed at a higher level in the future.

Take a moment right now to complete the following exercise.

What's the worst financial setback you've had in your life so far?

_____

_____

_____

What did you learn from this experience and how does that knowledge benefit you now?

_____

_____

_____

_____

How can you use that knowledge in the future to create a higher level of success in your life?

_____

_____

_____

_____

How does it feel to know that the worst thing that ever happened to you is now an *asset* toward your future financial success? If you consciously focus on what you learned and how it can benefit you in the future, you can effectively use it to your advantage in life.

PSYCHOLOGY: THE KEY TO YOUR SUCCESS

Along with these 12 wealth traits, successful people realize the inherent responsibility of owning their current condition. Many people fall into the trap of making excuses for not achieving financial abundance. They say things like, "I'm a spiritual person, I don't need money to make me happy," or "Money is evil." When you make excuses or settle for less, you're really

saying, "I'm afraid." You're either afraid of what will happen if you don't reach your goals or you're afraid of what will happen if you do!

Like handing any other area of your life, the ability to master your finances is just another way of saying to yourself, "I can grow in this area. I can and will become more." I'm not suggesting that you make money your most important value or make financial success your most important goal. Just remember that *you are where you are because of who you are.* If you feel frustrated with where you are financially, or even if you're doing relatively well but are hungry for more, your mental state is the place to start. What got you where you are will not get you where you want to go.

There are many vehicles available to help you make shifts in your direction. Life can do it for you by providing what I refer to as interventions, but that path can sometimes be longer and more painful. If this book does nothing else for you but cause you to look at the way you think, feel, and behave relative to money, I believe you will make the adjustments that will start you on a path to independence and fulfillment in this financial game. If you want to have wealth and financial success, you have to make it a course study. Books, audio programs (including CDs, radio, and podcasts), seminars, webinars, and coaching are all effective ways to start the process, and I've listed many valuable resources at the back of this book. I offer these suggestions with humility because I am on my own journey as well.

Let's quickly review what you've done so far: You completed the Take Count process. You found out where you are right now and evaluated how you're doing by using the Money Metrics evaluation process. You created your plan for total debt elimination by using the CREDiT Method, and you made positive adjustments to your thinking and attitude by doing the wealth traits exercises. In the next chapter, we'll look at how the wealthy stay out of debt and a fun tool I call the Cookie Jar Factor™. Let's get started.

I hear and I forget, I see and I remember, I do and I understand.

~ Chinese Proverb

CHAPTER EIGHT

The Power of Cookie Jars: Spend Smart and Enjoy It, Too

When I was a young boy in North Plainfield, New Jersey, my family and I lived in an upstairs apartment in my grandparents' home. I have explicit memories of a cookie jar on my grandmother's kitchen counter that was filled with cash instead of sweet treats. Whenever the ice cream man came around the neighborhood, Grandma would reach into that jar and give us money to buy something. This made my cousins and me very happy, and it made Grandma even happier to know she could give to us without impacting our other family goals. With six kids of their own and many grandchildren, my grandparents had expenses that added up fast. But Grandma knew she could treat us to something special from that jar because that's what the money was for. I don't know exactly how she and my grandfather managed their personal finances but I do know that she put that money aside so she could spend it however she wanted.

If you think about it, our grandparents didn't borrow much, if anything, other than a mortgage and a car loan. They certainly didn't spend the way we do now, and when they did spend, it was *planned*. They saved the money first, sometimes in a bank account and sometimes in coffee cans or cookie jars, and they marked that money for special use. My wife even claims that her grandmother stuffed money into the mattresses and under the staircase floorboards for future use.

When it comes to debt, most people face two issues: getting out and staying out. Getting out of debt (your debt elimination plan) has been the main focus of this book thus far. Staying out of debt (your major expense plan, also known as the Cookie Jar Factor) will be the focus of this chapter.

CREATING YOUR STAY-OUT-OF-DEBT PLAN

Debt comes from overspending, unexpected expenses, or impulse buying, so one way to eliminate debt is to *plan your expenses in advance* and decide what you can and cannot buy on impulse. Another way to alleviate debt is to stay associated to your critical result goals, which we'll work on together in part 3 of this book. In both cases, the key is to know the impact or consequence to your ultimate financial plan if you spend money frivolously or without a well-thought-out plan. Again I use the analogy of losing weight. If you don't keep it off, then your original plan (or psychology) was not enough.

For years I've been teaching the Cookie Jar Factor as a tool for staying out of debt. It's a simple process for identifying major expenses you know you'll face in the future and creating a plan *in advance* to set aside money for them on a regular basis. Much like an impound account for real estate property taxes and insurance, I define a cookie jar as an account into which you put money every paycheck, month, or quarter for a planned or anticipated future expense. With cookie jars, you have the opportunity to use the impound strategy for other expenses that don't occur monthly. By contributing consistently to your cookie jars, you can avoid borrowing money for major expenses like college educations, weddings, new cars, and vacations.

TYPES AND CLASSIFICATION OF COOKIE JARS

Following are some examples of cookie jars you may want to set up and strategies for organizing them. These examples are just that: examples. You may find that other expenses fit your situation. How you use the money is not important; what matters is developing the psychology of accumulating the money and then making the purchase so you stay away from borrowing and credit cards.

Jar #1: Automobile, Transportation

The purpose of this jar is to prepare for automobile and transportation needs such as a new or preferably used car, repairs, insurance, and registration. The money should be kept in an easily accessible, low-risk, short-term investment account. Money markets work well, since they have check-writing capabilities.

Jar #2: Home, Education, Medical

The purpose of this jar is to prepare for the major expenses of your home, education for yourself or your children, and any medical expenses. Your home expenses may include furniture, appliances, repairs, improvements, and remodels. In addition, this jar should include money for a new home, second home, or income property. Jar #2 should also include money for any planned education like college, private school, or adult education including seminars or personal development. In addition, it should provide for any antic-ipated medical or alternative medicine expenses. The money for these expenses should be kept in medium-term, low- to medium-risk investments like mutual funds or 529 plans.

Jar #3: Toys, Gifts, Vacations, Clothing, Pets

This jar is critical because these are areas where money can disap-pear and get you off track quickly. The purpose of this jar is to prepare and set aside money for any expenses relating to toys,

luxury items, and lifestyle purchases like computers, sporting goods, and activities such as concerts and weekend getaways. Also use this jar for gifts throughout the year for family and friends (birthdays, babies, weddings, holidays, etc). This money should be readily accessible in a money market account with check-writing capabilities, a regular bank savings account, or a short-term CD.

Jar #4: Insurance, Taxes, Professional Fees

The purpose of this jar is to prepare for your insurance and/or tax needs and any professional fees. These needs should include life, disability, auto, and homeowners insurances; projected federal and state income tax; and property taxes (if you don't have an impound account). You may also want to consider any professional expenses, like attorney's, tax preparer's, and investment advisor's fees. This money should be kept in an easily accessible, low-risk, short-term investment account. Money markets work well since they have check-writing capabilities.

The key with your cookie jars is to plan for any expenses that don't occur monthly. Now that you have an idea of what these expenses can be, take some time to create cookie jars for yourself and your family. Look at the following sample plan and then use the blank worksheet that follows to create your plan. (You didn't think I was going to let you out of this chapter without some follow-up work, now did you?) You can also download an online version of this worksheet at www.5MinuteDebtSolution.com.

Once you create your plan, we'll transfer the total amount you designate for cookie jars to a final draft of your Monthly Spending Plan, which you'll find in the next chapter.

TABLE 8.1 SAMPLE MAJOR EXPENSE PLAN
FOR FUTURE DEBT FREEDOM

My Name: Matt & Kate Bowman   **Gross monthly income:** $6,000

Today's date: 1/1/2008   **Percentage of income committed:** 10%

Jar (what is the money for?)	Account Institution	Goal Total	Current Balance	Amount Left to Save	Goal Deadline	Months to Achieve	Amount to Save per Month
Vacation	ABC Bank	$1,800	$200	$1,600	12/31/08	12	$134
Car repairs	ABC Bank	$800	$50	$750	6/30/08	6	$125
Patio furniture	Money Market	$1,200	$0	$1,200	12/31/08	12	$100
Educational seminar	Money Market	$2,000	$300	$1,700	3/31/09	15	$113
New clothes	ABC Bank	$600	$0	$600	6/30/08	6	$100
Cookie Jar Totals:		**$6,400**	**$550**	**$5,850**			**$572**

TABLE 8.2 MY MAJOR EXPENSE PLAN FOR FUTURE DEBT FREEDOM

My Name: _____

Today's date: _____

Gross monthly income: $ _____

Percentage of income committed: _____ %

Total amount: $ _____

Jar (what is the money for?)	Account Institution	Goal Total	Current Balance	Amount Left to Save	Goal Deadline	Months to Achieve	Amount to Save per Month
		$	$	$			$
		$	$	$			$
		$	$	$			$
		$	$	$			$
		$	$	$			$
		$	$	$			$
Cookie Jar Totals:		$	$	$			$

Creating your cookie jars is easy to do, and I can't think of a better strategy for staying out of debt (other than not spending at all). Unfortunately, things that are easy to do are usually easy *not* to do. The key point with your jars is to keep the commitments you make.

One couple I coach had plans to take a vacation to Bali for ten days. Sounds nice, right? The trip was going to cost them several thousand dollars and they were committed to paying cash and taking the trip within a certain time frame. However, the concept of cookie jars hadn't seized them yet. When they completed their game plans, including getting out of debt and saving for their future, they realized that they would have to either postpone the trip or come up with an alternative plan. They decided to take a less expensive trip to Cabo San Lucas and they put a plan in place that let them pay cash for the trip and go within their desired time frame. Because they got creative, they found a way to have their time off in a desirable locale without going into debt to do it. This is the creative, flexible approach of someone committed to a long-term, balanced plan for financial independence.

Remember that getting out of debt is not enough; you have to stay out. Commit to using the Cookie Jar Factor at least once a year, or preferably once each quarter, to make your plan for independence a reality.

A Final Note on Cookie Jars

In my seminars, one of the most frequent questions I get on this subject is, "Do I need to set up a separate account for each jar?" The answer is no. However, I typically recommend that you set up at least one separate (and preferably interest-bearing) account, like a money market, basic savings, or basic checking account. Then you can use a ledger or comment in your checking or savings register to note what the amounts are for. On the other hand, if having multiple accounts would make it easy for you to keep your commitments, then by all means go for it.

Once you have your account(s) set up, make the sum of the monthly commitment an *automatic transfer* into the account(s). We'll talk more specifically at the end of the book about automating your finances. But first let's get started on the next chapter where we'll work on creating your total spending plan for true financial success.

There is only one difference between the rich and poor and it is this: The rich save their money and spend what is left and the poor spend their money and save what is left.

~ Warren Buffett

CHAPTER NINE

Create Your Ultimate Spending Plan

This could be the most emotional chapter and subject of this entire book, but I promise not to mention the *B* word unless I must. I'm referring, of course, to a *budget*. Oops, sorry. I just said it, but it won't happen again.

Let's face it. No one wants to go on a budget, do they? (Darn it! Okay that will be the last time I use that word, I promise). In all seriousness, I want to introduce you to the concept of a *deliberate spending plan*, which I define as a plan for outgoing expenses that is in harmony with the rest of your financial plan. For the most part, other than things like unavoidable medical emergencies, overspending and a lack of planning are the only reasons people get into debt in the first place. Earlier we defined debt as the process of spending more than you earn and borrowing the difference. The operative word here is *spending*. To prevent debt from occurring, I recommend a deliberate spending plan.

We human beings have a natural tendency to move away from pain and move toward pleasure. I think it's fair to say that most people link being on the *B* word to pain, but as I mentioned earlier about shifting your vocabulary, I think most people want to be on a plan that they know will bring them what they ultimately want. In my one-on-one coaching, my clients grab onto this concept when we sit down and create this

exciting plan together. My goal here is to give you as much information as possible, using words on paper, to help you create a deliberate spending plan for yourself and your family, if that's important to you.

In this chapter I offer you a three-step process for creating a spending plan in total alignment with the objectives set forth in this book: getting out of debt as fast as possible, staying out of debt forever, and saving for your future independence. Your deliberate spending plan is where the rubber meets the road. This dynamic segment of your overall plan will determine whether you achieve your dreams or not. If income is the fuel for the fire, then your spending plan is either the water that squelches it or the gasoline that ignites it.

As you learned earlier, most people live their lives with the idea that when they make more money, *then* they will take action to get out of debt and save for the future. I'm here to tell you that this is the mind-set of failure. There's no question that more money can help, but only if you establish your winning game plan first; otherwise, more money will only make things worse.

Please remember these two concepts we discussed in chapter 7:

- You are where you are because of who you are.

- Money is a magnifier.

These two ideas may seem hard to grasp, but when you do grasp them everything can and will change for you. These two belief systems allow you to take total responsibility for where you are and to realize that no outside force (not even more money) will change your situation. Money truly can and in many cases does make things worse.

THREE STEPS TO SPENDING LESS

I promised you a three-step process, so let me give you the steps right here, and then I'll break them down one by one and give you some action items to put this important piece of your puzzle to work.

Step 1: Cut the fat — Diminish your wants and your perceptions of what you need.

Step 2: Shop and spend smart — Make sure you get the most value for your dollar.

Step 3: Spend with the long term in mind — Consider the big picture of each expense.

Step 1: Cut the Fat

We all have some fat to cut, especially if we haven't checked in with our spending recently. In your current spending pattern, what items can you trim or do without altogether? In a moment I want you to fill out the next worksheet. For the first column (Current Cost), you may refer back to the similar sheet in tables 2.6 and 2.7 if you feel you filled them out honestly and accurately. If not, you may want to start from scratch, because you need to start with figures that are real for you.

Ultimately I recommend that you enter every expense into a personal finance program such as Quicken or Microsoft Money so you can get an accurate expense report by category over at least 90 days. Most of us underestimate our spending, which is why we must monitor consistently. When I first used Quicken and started running my spending reports, I was astonished at the amount I was spending in some categories (such as dining and entertainment). If you're already using some type of program, then you already have access to this information.

All right, are you ready? Then go to table 9.1 and fill in the left-hand column (Current Monthly Cost). Once you've listed your current expenses to the best of your ability, go through them one by one and ask yourself the following questions:

1. Do I really want/need this expense anymore?

2. Does having this expense give me more joy than the negative impact of taking me away from my overall plan?

3. Would it feel better to lower or completely eliminate this expense?

4. What can I do to reduce or eliminate this expense while enjoying the process?

5. What need or emotion does the expense fulfill and can I meet this need less expensively or with no cost at all?

The next step will be to write down in the middle column (New/Ideal Monthly Cost) what you believe you can spend consistently on each expense based on your answers to the preceding questions. Please take the time to do this right now and then add it all up to see how much you can realistically cut from your expenses each month. I think you'll be surprised at what you can do if you put your heart into this exercise. I'll meet you on the other side and then we'll look at the next step and see what you can do with all the money you'll save when you follow this plan.

TABLE 9.1 CUT THE FAT & SPEND SMART EXERCISE

Category of Expense	Current Monthly Cost	New/Ideal Monthly Cost	Spend Smart
1. **Rent or Property Taxes** (if you own your home, list property taxes only):	$	$	$
2. **Food—Groceries Only** (include food and household groceries):	$	$	$
3. **Clothing/Grooming** (include basic clothing, haircuts, makeup):	$	$	$
4. **Auto/Transportation** (service, fuel, parking, registration):	$	$	$
5. **Insurances** (life, disability, medical, HMO, auto, PMI, legal, home):	$	$	$
6. **Utilities** (gas/electric, cable, phone, cell phone, water, trash, sewer):	$	$	$
7. **Minimum Debt Payments** (from table 2.4):	$	$	$
Business Expenses (any un-reimbursed business expenses):	$	$	$
Child Expenses (day care, nanny, baby-sitter, child care or support, camps):	$	$	$
Clubs/Organizations (dues for athletic club/gym, magazines, environment, etc):	$	$	$
Contribution (political, charity, church, tithing, and donations):	$	$	$
Education (college, continuing education, personal growth seminars, books/tapes, or CDs):	$	$	$

Electronics/Technology (audiovisual, computer, PDA/cell phones, pager, etc.):	$	$	$
Food—Dining Out (include restaurants, snacks, coffees, vending machines):	$	$	$
Financial/Banking (include broker fees, annual fees, service fees, ATMs, etc.):	$	$	$
Fun/Entertainment (include concerts, shows, movies, clubs, videos, CDs):	$	$	$
Gifts (include birthdays, anniversaries, holidays, weddings, babies, etc.):	$	$	$
Grooming (include hair color, salon services, pedicures/manicures):	$	$	$
Habits (cigarettes/tobacco, alcohol, gambling, etc.):	$	$	$
Hobbies/Activities (sporting goods, golf camping, scuba, skiing, painting, etc.):	$	$	$
Household Groceries (toiletries, paper goods, cleansers, laundry, etc.):	$	$	$
Household Items (furniture, appliances, decor items, kitchen/bath accessories):	$	$	$
Household Maintenance (windows, carpets, paint, etc.):	$	$	$
Household Staff/Support (security service, maids, gardener, pool, etc.):	$	$	$
Legal/Professional Fees (attorneys, CPAs, financial advisors, etc.):	$	$	$

Luxury Items (yacht/boat, airplane, limousine, spa retreats, etc.):	$	$	$
Medical/Dental/Alternative (glasses, prescriptions, massage, chiropractor, acupuncture, herbs/supplements, etc.):	$	$	$
Personal Accessories (jewelry, purses, hats, sunglasses, etc.):	$	$	$
Pet Care (veterinarian, food, toys, supplies, etc.):	$	$	$
Rentals/Properties (mortgage payment and all expenses, upkeep, etc.):	$	$	$
Toys (motorcycles, boats, jet skis, etc.):	$	$	$
Travel/Vacations (airfare, hotels, time-shares, car rental, activities, etc.):	$	$	$
Any Other Expenses:	$	$	$
Subtotal All Expenses:	$	$	$
Total Savings from Cutting These Expenses: (subtract the New/Ideal Total from the Current Cost)	$	$	

I can only assume that you have cut something here. Even a small amount can add up to big changes over time when redirected appropriately. If you cut a significant amount, I truly congratulate you.

Once you've completed your Cut the Fat exercise, you need to decide how you will redirect the money you've cut from your expenses. However, before you make any decisions about redirecting funds, I want

you to go through one more process that may add even more to your total of extra money each month. You may have to take some time with this next process to do some investigating and shopping for a better value. Let me present it to you and then you can decide whether you want to focus on more changes now or simply add the changes you've already identified to your overall spending plan.

Remember, accomplishing your goals is a journey, so this is a new beginning for you, not the end. You can come back to the exercises again and again when you feel it is important to reassess. My wife and I just did this process again this year and we're very excited about our new plan. Like many people, we got off track in a few areas but we made some important changes (cuts) by going through this process.

Step 2: Shop and Spend Smart

I'm not talking about the ordinary kind of shopping where you spend money, I'm referring to the kind where you spend less or get a better value by investigating and comparing offers. The idea here is to get the most out of each dollar you spend and to use every available resource when making a purchase.

Now that you've gone through your monthly expenses item by item with the idea of cutting or reducing what you don't need, I invite you to do it once again using the far right column (Spend Smart) while answering the questions that follow. If you come up against an item you're not sure about, you may want to write the word *research* in the Spend Smart column and schedule time in the near future to see what better value you might be able to get.

Let's get started right now by going through each line item in the preceding worksheet and answering the following evaluation questions. As you ask yourself each question, if you believe you can lower the overall amount you spend, then write your new answer (dollar figure) in the Spend Smart column.

1. Am I really getting the most for my money with this expense?
2. Have I attempted to get a better price or terms on this expense?
3. Have I really done my homework to get the best deal?
4. Where can I get the same or better quality for less?
5. If I buy this at a different time, will it be less popular or possibly on sale?

In following this step, one strategy my wife and I use is to buy many of our clothes out of season when they are priced lower. Remember my story from chapter 3 about the jacket I wanted for Christmas? Big businesses count on our sense of urgency to buy things within a certain period of time, and they capitalize on this trait by keeping prices higher. We have to beat them at their game because little expenses like these over 20 or 30 years can have a significant impact on our personal finances.

If you were able to cut even more with this third step, congratulations! Subtotal your Spend Smart amount, then add it to your total savings from step 1 and enter it into the bottom right-hand box of table 9.1. Keep this number handy because you'll come back to it as you rewrite your new total plan.

My preference is that you do one of two things with this amount:

- Consider beefing up either your DEA Factor (the consistent amount of money you pay over and above your minimum monthly debt payments) or the amount of money you put toward savings for the future.
- Consider increasing a combination of both.

The key with this piece of your plan is to make sure you have some type of system to monitor and measure what you really spend so you stay on track. The last thing you want to do is take time to create a plan and then fail to follow through. Again, if you don't have some type of computer program for this, get one now as it is critical.

Step 3: Spend with the Long Term in Mind

My wife has always dreamed of having a swimming pool in her own backyard. Of course, as "her man" I want to be able to provide and make dreams come true for her and our family. Being the planner I am, I started crunching the numbers to see what it would take to make this happen. Since we have very young children (ages five and three, as I write this book), we would not want to build a pool until they're a bit older for safety reasons, which gives me a few years to make it happen. I began to investigate and talk with neighbors who had their own pool. I asked many questions about what the pool cost and what they got for their money. Probably the most important question I asked was how much they pay each month to maintain and heat the pool. The numbers shocked me. Not because it was a huge monthly number, but because we plan to live in our home for about 20 years.

Keeping the long term in mind, I started adding up the numbers, factored in inflation, and estimated for higher-end maintenance that the pool will surely need when it gets older. The numbers became astonishing. Again, I had to step outside the mind-set of low monthly payments and consider the long-term impact over the many years we would have this product. Needless to say, our community pool is starting to look very good to us for the few dollars it costs per visit. Had I not considered the long-term impact, I might have put a plan into place to fund the initial expense. Fortunately, I was not shortsighted and I avoided that trap.

Earlier we spoke about wealth traits, and of course there are more than 12 of them. In reality, there are dozens if not hundreds but I wanted to give you what I felt were among the most important for someone beginning to build a solid foundation for wealth. Here's another one to add to the list: Wealthy people see a dollar not for what it's worth to them in the moment, but for what it will be worth to them in the future. This is another way of saying that successful people focus on the long term and they have a vision for every dollar they earn and spend. Wealthy people approach the game as more than consumers; they approach it as businesspeople or investors. I'm not speaking of being cheap or miserly (where do you think the word *miserable* comes from?) but rather of being a long-term thinker and investor.

Let's take a look at some scenarios where a simple shift in focus and approach can make a measurable difference in your financial destiny. Please know that it is not my intent with the following scenarios to make any specific stock recommendations or give you any investment ideas, but rather to make the point that *one decision can impact your financial destiny,* no matter how small that decision may appear in the moment.

AN IPOD OR AN APPLE?

In October 2001, Apple, Inc. introduced the iPod, a portable digital music device about the size of a pack of cigarettes that held approximately 100 albums worth of music (as if I needed to describe it in detail). By April 2007, Apple had sold 100 million units. Let's take a look at the difference between person A, the consumer, and person B, the investor. Remember, this is just one scenario and one decision.

Person A bought the iPod when it was announced for the introductory price of $399. He got his five-gigabyte unit and quickly downloaded some music. He enjoyed his iPod for a year or two, but the whereabouts of his original version are now unknown, most likely in an electronic graveyard somewhere, and he has since bought one or two different upgrades of the same product, spending hundreds of dollars more.

Person B decided to hold off on this electronic miracle for a few years and instead took his $399 and bought Apple stock (NASDAQ symbol: AAPL) for $10.65 per share, acquiring approximately 37.5 shares. On February 28, 2005, at a stock price of approximately $84.61, the stock split two for one, giving Person B a total of 75 shares. In May 2007 his holdings climbed to $8,546.25 when the stock reached $113.95 per share. Person B can now sell two shares of his stock to purchase his iPod nano, which actually holds nearly twice as much music, is nearly 10 times smaller, and costs approximately $199—half the price of its first-generation counterpart—and still hold 73 shares of this leader of its industry.

IT'S JUST A PACK OF CIGARETTES, RIGHT?

Couple A smoked three packs of cigarettes per day for 46 years. They spent approximately $33,190 for their "smokes" during that period and constantly argued that they had no money to save or invest.

Couple B decided not to smoke anymore. Instead, they purchased Phillip Morris stock with the same amount of money, dollar cost averaging the stock over that same 46-year period. Not only will they be in better health, but after having reinvested all dividends and selling the stock at its peak, they will also have that same $33,190 in stock that is now worth approximately $2.2 million.

BUY A CAR OR A CAR COMPANY?

Person A bought a Subaru in 1967 for approximately $6,000. He is not certain where that car is today because he sold it for a few hundred dollars and bought another car. Person B instead purchased $6,000 worth of Subaru stock at about $2 per share in 1967. At its peak of $167, it was worth over half a million dollars.

IS IT REALLY THE REAL THING?

On average, each child in the United States consumes three 12-ounce sodas per day. If instead of buying these sodas, they invested in Coca-Cola stock, they would have a lot of money. Three sodas per day add up to 1,095 per year. At a vending machine cost of 75 cents, that equates to more than $820 per year. If they had saved that money and invested in Coca-Cola stock at the end of each year for the past five years, they would now have over 117 shares of stock. They would have invested a total of $4,100, which would have been worth $8,292 at its peak in May 1999.

You can never underestimate the power of one decision or one change to your spending plan. David Bach, a friend and associate of mine who has written several fantastic books on financial success (and helped coach me on the success of this one), calls this the latte factor. Bach asserts that people are drinking their entire retirement portfolio (critical mass) *one coffee drink at a time, one day at a time* because they aren't focused on the long term. Before you make a purchase—any purchase—please take a moment to think about the impact over time of this expense and whether your money and financial future would be better served by choosing not to make the purchase now.

Okay, enough about debt and enough about spending. Are you ready for the fun, juicy, and brighter side of this book? I'm talking about *goals*—really taking a look at what you want and what it will take for you to have the financial independence we've been talking so much about. This is my favorite part because I always see people light up when they create this part of their plan and integrate it with the belief of possibility. Let's get started.

PART THREE

Invest in Your Long-Term Dreams

It concerns us to know the purpose we seek in life, for then like archers aiming at a definite mark, we shall be more likely to attain what we want.

~ Aristotle

CHAPTER TEN

Set Clear and Compelling Financial Goals

When I was between the ages of 23 and 26 years old, I worked two jobs for two and a half years. I worked for the consumer lender I spoke about earlier, and I also waited tables at night and on weekends in a local restaurant. I worked the equivalent of eight days a week and I swiftly saved $10,000 cash in the bank. I had much more money both in income and in assets than most of my friends at the time and I was feeling on top of the world. Then something interesting happened.

Just before I left my career as a lender/collector, I put down $5,000 on a brand-new 1988 Toyota Celica. Soon after leaving my job, with much free time on my hands, I went to Europe for six and a half weeks and blew the other $5,000. It took me six months to spend everything I had saved in those 30 months of working. If that wasn't enough, I went into quite a bit of debt because I wasn't making much money but I kept the same lifestyle as when I worked two jobs. I believe to this day that the primary reason I did this was because I had no greater goal for that $10,000. The money was not part of anything bigger in my mind, and with no financial plan in place I squandered it like there was no tomorrow.

In this chapter I want to make sure you create a plan for tomorrow and identify the greater goals that will pull you in the direction of your long-term vision and dreams. Getting out of debt and staying out of debt

are both important goals but I doubt that they will get you up early in the morning and keep you up late at night with any sense of passion and purpose. The final piece in your fundamental plan for success is to set clear and compelling financial goals.

In the next few pages, you'll learn about three different kinds of financial goals, decide what you want, and discover what you need financially to have the lifestyle you desire and deserve. You'll create a wish list of all your goals and dreams. You'll also discover the emotional reasons behind your objectives by writing out a statement of your identity (who you are and will become) and purpose (why you want these specific results). If you have enough compelling and emotional reasons *why* you want something, you'll figure out how to get it.

A NOTE ABOUT LONG-TERM FINANCIAL PLANNING

Before we get into the financial goals themselves, we should discuss a few factors that play a significant role in financial success. I want to keep this chapter as simple as possible but I would be remiss to leave out at least a few of the factors that can and more than likely will impact your overall plan. The first of these is that you can approach the ultimate achievement of your goals in one of three ways:

- **Option 1: You plan to spend most or all of the money you have accumulated.** You may have seen this choice proudly summed up on the back of a Motor Coach rolling down the highway on a bumper sticker that says, WE'RE SPENDING OUR CHILDREN'S INHERITANCE. Yes, option 1 is about using your savings to fund your golden years.

- **Option 2: You live purely off the investment gains you receive from your critical mass of savings and investments.** This option is critically dependent on your ability to either invest successfully to create an ongoing income or to have so much money that it doesn't really matter what type of return you get. In this option, you live from the blended return on your investments (the total gains and losses from all the investments you have), taking into consideration your real return (the net gains on your investments after accounting for capital gains and other taxes).

- **Option 3: You plan to live off a combination of the two.** You may decide to chip away at your savings mass over time and combine it with the income you produce for a better lifestyle along the way.

The main concern with options 1 and 3 is the possibility of outliving your money. Option 2 creates a more conservative plan but requires you to be diligent about your investment income and to have a plan for inheritance (meaning the proper care and allocation of the money you leave behind).

While all three options assume a level of self-reliance and do not consider pensions and/or government assistance, they can be combined with pension or social security income. However, my goal for you would be that you treat this type of additional income as icing on the cake rather than relying on it. This is the essence of financial independence. As I write this book, the current prediction is that social security funding will be bankrupt within the next 14 years, depending on which calculation or prediction you listen to. I don't know the answer to this (nor am I convinced that many professionals do, either); however, I think it would be wise to create a conservative plan that does not rely on government assistance if you want to have any quality of life. If you do receive some or all of your social security benefits you can either increase your lifestyle, leave more behind for your family, or give more away to charities or social organizations you support.

In addition to considering these three options for achieving your goals, you must also consider another important factor: inflation. As you know, I am not an economist and I cannot make predictions about inflation, but I can tell you that inflation has historically grown at a rate of approximately 4% per year over the past 20 years. If this indicator is a projection of what will happen in the future, then you need to plan for this as well. Some organizations will tell you that *deflation* in our lifetime is also a strong possibility, and if you're prepared, it can work to your advantage by allowing you to increase your lifestyle or prolong your money. In either case, you need to be prepared for the probable reality that a dollar in the year 2028 or beyond will buy much less than a dollar today.

To put this into perspective, imagine that you retired 10 or 20 years ago. What would have cost you a dollar in 1997 would cost you $1.29 in 2007. What would have cost you a dollar in 1987 would cost you $1.87 in 2007, nearly twice as much.

Here are some examples of what costs will be 10 and 20 years from now at 4% inflation:

TABLE 10.1 COSTS IN 10 AND 20 YEARS AT 4% INFLATION

Item	Present Cost	Cost in 10 Years	Cost in 20 Years
Gallon of Gas	$2.80	$4.14	$6.14
Movie Ticket	$9.00	$13.25	$19.75
Suit or Outfit	$500	$740	$1,095
Computer	$1,200	$1,776	$2,629
Car	$25,000	$37,000	$54,778
Home	$300,000	$444,073	$657,336

It's also important to note that certain items inflate faster than others, so your end result can also depend on where you spend your money, but the overall trend has always been up.

With all of this planning and trying to figure out how much you need and what it will take, I'm reminded of a quote by the brilliant Warren Buffett who said, "I'd rather be approximately right than precisely wrong." It appears to me that many people don't take these small actions to plan or think about the future because they're afraid of not being precisely right, which can be a formula for disaster. As the old saying goes, *if you're failing to plan, you're planning to fail.*

THREE TYPES OF FINANCIAL GOALS

There are three types of financial goals: independence goals (IGs), pathway goals, and lifestyle goals. The first type, independence goals, are specific and generally big, long-term targets. They represent a dollar amount and a lifestyle attached to that amount. They are commonly referred to as your nest egg or retirement goals. Being *financially independent* means creating choice and lifestyle rather than having them imposed upon you. Since independence goals are critical to your long-term success, the majority of this chapter will be focused on them.

Independence Goals

There are three levels of IGs, and we'll examine each one in the next few pages. We'll also take time to calculate yours, using a very simple process. Please note that these exercises are meant to help you come up with some targets that will compel you to take the daily actions that will create new momentum in your financial life and give you a sense of certainty that you can achieve your goals. You need to have these targets to shoot for so that when you save something—even

if it's just a few dollars—you know it's part of something bigger: your independence goals. You don't want to work hard to save a sum of money only to blow it (that's a technical term for frivolous spending) down the road because you have no longer-term plan or greater purpose for it. Don't worry about how you'll accumulate these totals now. Later in this chapter we'll deal with "chunking down" your goals, so you'll know what you have to do over a period of time to get to this number. This piece is about *what* and *why*.

Figure 10.1 illustrates the three levels of IGs (yes, it's another ladder). Look it over and then we'll break each level down so you understand the definition and concept.

Figure 10.1 Independence Goals: Your Ladder for Long-Term Financial Success

IG #3: Financial Abundance for Life

IG #2: Financial Independence for Life

IG #1: Financial Assurance for Life

Financial Assurance, 5 Years

Financial Assurance, 6–12 months

Independence Goal #1: Financial Assurance

Think of IGs as a ladder for financial success. This ladder has five rungs or levels of success. The three bottom rungs make up the first level of goals: financial assurance. Having *financial assurance* simply means having an assured amount of money that will cover your expenses for a predefined period of time. By meeting seven basic needs, you can be assured of your ability to cover these expenses, starting with 6 to 12 months, building to 5 to 10 years, and eventually for the remainder of your life. Some people refer to this as an emergency fund, and at some level it is. You also have to think long term and realize that *this is the foundation of your independence and retirement.* If emergencies keep coming up you can never get to the next level or rung of the ladder.

Let's look at a sample worksheet in table 10.2 and then you can calculate your financial assurance goals using the blank worksheet that follows (table 10.3). If you like, you can refer back to the Monthly Expense sheets in chapter 2; however, please make sure that, if you choose to do this, these sheets were filled out accurately.

TABLE 10.2 SAMPLE SEVEN CRITICAL EXPENSES FOR FINANCIAL ASSURANCE

1. Rent or Property Taxes (if you own, list property taxes only):	$700
2. Food–Groceries only (include food and household groceries):	$800
3. Clothing/Grooming (include basic clothing, haircuts, makeup):	$300
4. Auto/Transportation (service, fuel, parking, registration):	$400
5. Insurances (life, disability, medical, HMO, auto, PMI, legal, home/hazard):	$300
6. Utilities (gas/electric, cable, phone, cell phone, water, trash, sewer):	$250
7. Total Minimum Monthly Payments (from the Debts and Liabilities worksheet, table 2.4):	$1,900
Total Seven Critical Expenses (Total of your Seven Critical Expenses):	$4,650
Amount I need for 6 months of basic living expenses (monthly amount multiplied by 6):	$27,900
Amount I need for 5 years (monthly amount x 60):	$279,000
Amount I need for life (monthly amount x 12 and then divided by .06 blended return):	$930,000

Before you calculate your own critical monthly expenses, I want to point out two things with regard to the preceding example. The first relates to the seventh critical expense, labeled "Total Minimum Monthly Payments." Please keep in mind that when you are debt free (including your mortgage) and living on a cash basis (which is a top objective of this

book), the amount of money you need to be financially assured or independent will *decrease* significantly. To make your plan conservative, however, we'll continue calculating your goals with your currently monthly debt payments included.

The second important point relates to the last row, labeled "Amount I need for life." To calculate this amount, the worksheet instructs you to divide your desired annual income by .06. I used this figure as a default "real" return on investments (ROI less capital gains taxes); it represents a blended and real return of 6%. For example, if you wanted $75,000 per year you would simply divide that by 6% (.06) to come up with $1,250,000 to generate this income. You may want to increase the blended return amount if feel you can do better (if you are a savvy investor or have a great stockbroker or financial planner), or you may want to decrease it if you don't feel comfortable with this rate of return. Remember, *the lower the rate of return, the more money you need* (critical mass of savings and investments) to generate the income that will provide this lifestyle. This principle also works in reverse: *the higher your rate of return, the lower amount of savings mass you may need.*

Are you ready to calculate your financial assurance goal? Please fill in this next worksheet and I'll see you on the other side. Again, if you choose to use the figures from chapter 2, please feel free to do so.

Table 10.3 My Financial Assurance Goal

1. Rent or Property Taxes (if you own, list property taxes only):	$
2. Food–Groceries only (include food and household groceries):	$
3. Clothing/Grooming (include basic clothing, haircuts, makeup):	$
4. Auto/Transportation (service, fuel, parking, registration):	$
5. Insurances (life, disability, medical, HMO, auto, PMI, legal, home/hazard):	$
6. Utilities (gas/electric, cable, phone, cell phone, water, trash, sewer):	$
7. Total Minimum Monthly Payments (from the Debts and Liabilities worksheet, table 2.4):	$
Total Seven Critical Expenses	$
Amount I need for _____ months of basic living expenses (monthly amount multiplied by 6):	$
Amount I need for 5 years (monthly amount x 60):	$
Amount I need for life (monthly amount x 12 and then divided by .06 blended return):	$

Independence Goal #2: Financial Independence

Financial independence means you've met your seven critical needs and you can continue to fund the additional expenses listed in your discretionary expense sheets in chapter 2 without having to work. It's important to note here that some expenses you have now (like child care or a large

home) you may not have in the future, and some expenses you don't have now or have in small amounts (like medical expenses) you may have more of in the future.

When you achieve this level, you can essentially maintain the same, similar, or even better lifestyle than you have today without working because your income is generated from your critical mass of savings and investments. I have offered two ways to calculate this number. One is to fill out a detailed worksheet like you've been doing throughout this book, and another is a shortcut way of getting to the number quickly and easily. I recommend that you utilize the worksheets so you think about each expense individually and know that your total is solid and realistic. However, if you want to utilize the shortcut method, all I truly care about is the outcome: that you come up with a compelling, realistic number that you believe you can achieve. Let's calculate your financial independence goal.

TABLE 10.4 MY DISCRETIONARY MONTHLY EXPENSES

Business Expenses (any un-reimbursed business expenses):	$
Child Expenses (day care, nanny, babysitter, child care or support, camp):	$
Clubs/Organizations (dues for gym, athletic club, magazines, environmental, community, etc):	$
Contribution (political, charity, church, tithing, donations):	$
Education (college, continuing education, personal growth seminars, books/CDs):	$
Electronics/Technology (computers, audiovisual, PDA, cell phones, pagers, MP3 players, etc.):	$
Food/Dining Out (restaurants, snacks, coffee, vending machines):	$
Financial/Banking (broker fees, annual fees, service fees, ATM, etc.):	$
Fun/Entertainment (concerts, shows, movies, clubs, video rental, CDs):	$
Gifts (birthdays, anniversaries, holidays, weddings, babies, etc.):	$
Habits (cigarettes/tobacco, alcohol, gambling, etc.):	$
Hobbies/Activities (sporting, camping, golf, scuba, skiing, painting, etc.):	$
Household Groceries (toiletries, paper goods, cleansers, laundry, etc.):	$
Household Items (furniture, appliances, decorative items, kitchen/bath):	$

Household Maintenance (windows, carpets, paint, etc.):	$
Household Staff/Support (security service, maid, gardener, pool, etc.):	$
Legal/Professional Fees (attorneys, CPAs, financial advisors, etc.):	$
Luxury Items (yacht/boat, airplane, limousine, spa retreats, etc.):	$
Medical/Dental/Alternative (glasses, prescriptions, massage, chiropractor, acupuncture, herbs/supplements, etc.):	$
Personal Accessories (jewelry, purses, hats, sunglasses, etc.):	$
Pet Care (veterinarian, food, toys, supplies, etc.):	$
Rentals/Properties (mortgage payment and all expenses, upkeep, etc.):	$
Toys (motorcycles, boats, jet skis, etc.):	$
Travel/Vacations (airfare, hotels, timeshares, car rental, activities, etc.):	$
Any Other Expenses:	$
Subtotal Discretionary Expenses:	$
Total All Monthly Expenses (Seven Critical Expenses plus Discretionary Expenses):	$
Critical Mass Amount I Need for Financial Independence: (Total Monthly Expenses x 12 and divided by .06 Real Return)	$

For those of you who say, "I'm not filling out another darn worksheet," here's a shortcut way to arrive at this amount. Simply decide on the monthly amount of money that would cover all of your expenses and make you feel (and believe) you would be independent. This number could replace your current income, it could be more if you do not currently have the income you desire, or it could be less if you have an income that exceeds your future lifestyle desires. Now multiply that number by 12 and then divide it by .06 (or a real return you know you can achieve). For example:

Monthly income desired: $6,000

Annual income desired: $72,000 (monthly amount x 12)

Critical mass amount: $1,200,000 (annual income divided by .06)

Now you do it:

Monthly income desired: $_____

Annual income desired: $_____

Critical mass amount: $_____

Independence Goal #3: Financial Abundance

Financial abundance means having the ability to do what you want, when you want, without having to worry about it. Some might call this being filthy rich but it simply means having your *dream lifestyle* by living purely off the income generated by your personal investments.

Not everyone will choose to reach this level. Some people are satisfied with financial independence or unwilling to part with the resources needed to achieve financial abundance. Others may prefer to donate any monies above and beyond financial independence to charity because they rank contribution higher on their personal list of values than they rank the feeling financial abundance would give. Not everyone wants to be a Bill Gates, a Donald Trump, or an Oprah Winfrey—and that's okay. These

people are amazing role models, but their levels of financial success and lifestyle are not for everyone. The point is to decide what *you* ultimately want and to make that your aspiration.

If you're unclear, here are some targets that may come to mind when you achieve this level:

- Take extended vacations (trip around the world, rent a home for the summer, etc.)
- Give scholarships
- Purchase second, third, or even fourth homes
- Own multiple vehicles
- Own boats, yachts
- Have an automobile collection
- Support other family members
- Own a private island
- Buy a private jet or airplane
- Own an art collection
- Own a sports franchise
- Own a high-rise building

For those of you who do not seek this type of lifestyle, skip ahead to the next section. For those of you who dream big, let's take some time to figure out what it will take. To help you get started, you may want to get a few magazines that cater to the highly affluent and see what these luxury items cost. Let me offer one quick word of caution. Before you start adding luxury items to your plan, make sure each one is something you really want for yourself and your family. Since this is a book about getting out of debt and staying out of debt, you must also assume that you will pay cash for these types of expenses or at least finance or leverage them in a highly intelligent way.

To get to the level of financial abundance, you need to figure out what additional money it will take to fund this level of lifestyle, break it down to monthly costs, and factor it into your plan as you did in the previous exercises. When you've identified the expenses you'll incur in your life of financial abundance, please add them to the blank spaces in the following worksheet. Then calculate the total additional amount you'll need for this level.

TABLE 10.5 SAMPLE FINANCIAL ABUNDANCE GOALS

Financial Abundance Goal	Approximate Monthly Cost
Total Monthly Amount I Need for Financial Independence (from table 10.4):	$8,000
Second Home in Southwest	$3,000
Annual Trip around the World	$6,000
Third Home in Hawaii	$4,000
Collector Car	$500
Fly Immediate Family to Hawaii Annually	$1,000
	$
	$
Total Monthly Amount I Need for Financial Abundance	$22,500
Total Critical Mass Amount I Need to Create Financial Abundance (Monthly Amount above x 12 divided by .06 Blended Return)	$4,500,000

TABLE 10.6 MY FINANCIAL ABUNDANCE GOALS

Abundance Goal	Approximate Monthly Cost
Total Monthly Amount I Need for Financial Independence (from table 10.4):	$
	$
	$
	$
	$
	$
	$
	$
Total Monthly Amount I Need for Financial Abundance	$
Total Critical Mass Amount I Need to Create Financial Abundance (Monthly Amount above x 12 divided by .06 Blended Return)	$

Declaration of Financial Independence

The final step in this segment is to capture your three independence goals onto one page I call your *declaration of financial independence*. In addition, I want you to give yourself a specific date as a deadline for achieving them. You may want to think of this date in five-year chunks, like 10, 15, or 20 years from now. Your declaration of financial independence doesn't have to be perfect and you don't need to worry about exactly how you're going to accomplish your goals yet. Just set the date and we'll figure out how later.

At some point you may want to meet with a coach like myself or a professional planner to help you assess what you're doing to get to this place called financial abundance or independence. As I mentioned earlier, there are many factors that will determine when you get there, including your income, the amount you commit to save each month and year, the blended real return you receive, inflation, and any unpredictable changes that may affect any or all of the above.

You may want to photocopy your declaration page or tear it out of your book and put it in your day planner or other location where you will see it every day (such as the bathroom mirror, wall or your refrigerator). If you like, you can download an attractive PDF file of this page from my Web site.

My Declaration of Financial Independence

These are the desired outcomes I commit to from this day forth. I promise myself to be committed, flexible, disciplined, and focused, and to do whatever it takes to make these dreams come true for me and my family. Today, I declare my independence from work and I commit to building the foundation of financial well-being that will provide the freedom, prosperity, and quality of life I truly desire and deserve.

My Independence Goals

The amount I need for lifetime *financial assurance* is $_____.

I will have this amount by the year _____.

The amount I need for *financial independence* is $_____.

I will have this amount by the year _____.

The amount I need for *financial abundance* is $_____.

I will have this amount by the year _____.

Date _____   Signed _____

It is your birthright to have financial independence.
You deserve it and you can achieve it!

— Chris P. Hendrickson

Pathway Goals

Pathway goals, the second type of financial goals, are more short-term in nature. These specific goals will take you in the direction of your IGs by adding to and growing your net worth and your critical mass. In other words, they are the steppingstones that accumulate and lead you in the direction of your long-term targets. Here are some examples of pathway goals:

- Weekly, monthly, quarterly goals
- Investment goals (e.g., stocks, trading, real estate, ROI, etc.)
- Yearly or annual goals
- Getting-out-of-debt goals
- Staying-out-of-debt goals
- Savings goals
- One-, five-, and ten-year goals
- Income-producing goals
- Spending goals
- Business goals
- Asset allocation goals
- Protection goals (e.g., starting an estate plan, writing a will, or getting insurance)
- Tax-related goals
- Creative goals (writing this book was a creative goal for me)

Your independence goals are imperative. Pathway goals are a way of breaking down your IGs into something you can do this year, this quarter, this month, this week, and *today* to bring your long-term goals to fruition.

Your pathway goals will ultimately get you to your destination. We'll brainstorm these in a moment, but first let's look at the third type of goals.

Lifestyle Goals

Lifestyle goals, the third type of financial goals, actually take you further away from the first two types. Lifestyle goals inherently inhibit your ability to accomplish your pathway and independence goals because they require you to *spend* money rather than *save and invest* it. They are, however, sometimes essential to enjoying life, as long as they are approached with honesty, balance, and planning. This book is not about saving, saving, saving and never getting to enjoy your life; that would be a lifestyle of greed or misery. This book is about helping you save, invest, grow, and protect your money while spending a portion of it on enjoyment and a balanced quality of life for yourself and your family. This is called true wealth, and you can have it when you take the time to figure out what you want and need and you keep your ultimate long-term plan in mind while spending. These are some examples of lifestyle goals:

- Vacation and travel goals
- Clothing
- Recreation
- Education goals
- Health and wellness goals
- Toys
- Celebration or party goals
- Vehicles
- Credit goals
- Contribution goals

- Bigger home or remodeling

- Gift goals

- Second home (not as a rental)

- Creativity goals

BRAINSTORM, CAPTURE, AND REALIZE YOUR GOALS

Now that you understand the types of goals, it's time to identify yours. There are two steps in the goal-setting process:

1. Brainstorming every goal you can possibly think of

2. Creating a hierarchy with detailed descriptions of each goal, including what, how, why, and when you will achieve it

There's a big difference between setting a goal and *achieving* a goal. After you set a goal, you must give your mind as much detailed information about it as possible so you may direct its course with your specific action plan. Then you back it up with many emotionally charged reasons why you must achieve the goal. Here are five tips to help you with the goal-setting process:

- Include a balance of all three types of goals (independence, pathway, and lifestyle). You don't want to have two pages of lifestyle goals and no pathway goals, or vice versa.

- Play some of your favorite music or go to a favorite place— something or somewhere uplifting or inspirational that will put you in a resourceful and powerful state of mind.

- Open your imagination and induce creative thoughts and ideas, putting yourself in a mind-set of no limitations.

- If you have a journal, other type of book, or a computer program, you may prefer to write and capture in these.

- Remember, now is not the time to analyze how you will achieve your goals. Anything is possible in this portion of the process. Think big!

Now I'd like you to take 5 to 10 minutes to brainstorm and capture as many goals as you can possibly think of onto the following pages. Ready, set, go!

TABLE 10.7 BRAINSTORMING WORKSHEET

Goal (Brief Description)	Type (Lifestyle, Pathway, or IG)	Time Frame (Years)

Goal (Brief Description)	Type (Lifestyle, Pathway, or IG)	Time Frame (Years)

My Top 5 Goals

The next step will be to glance briefly at all the goals you listed and put an asterisk next to the five you feel are critical to work toward or accomplish in the coming year. Then take a few moments and write them below in order of importance as your top five goals for this year. Remember to have a balance of the different types of goals.

These are the top five goals I am committed to achieving in the next 12 months:

1. _____

   _____

2. _____

   _____

3. _____

   _____

4. _____

   _____

5. _____

   _____

CREATING OR REDEFINING YOUR FINANCIAL IDENTITY

The purpose of a goal is not so much what you will get but rather *who you will become* during the process of achieving it. Take a few moments right now to write down *who you would have to become in order to achieve all that you want* (e.g., I must become a student of financial success, I must be focused and disciplined, I must be aware of where my money goes each month, I must always spend less than I earn, I must consistently measure and monitor my goals).

Who must I become in order to achieve all that I want?

_____

_____

_____

_____

_____

_____

CREATING YOUR FINANCIAL MISSION OR PURPOSE STATEMENT

In the introduction to this book I said that this was going to be your playbook for financial success. There may not be a more important part of your playbook than to sit down and think about *why* you are playing

this game. Remember, *reasons come first!* When you get down to it, you can only do two things with your money: you can keep it (save and invest) or you can part with it (spend). Take two minutes to write down all the reasons you must (not should, but *must*) save and invest more of your money in order to reach your goals and dreams, and more important, your own independence.

Take a moment right now to think about why you want and must succeed at this game. Who else does this decision impact?

_____

_____

_____

_____

_____

_____

_____

_____

CREATING YOUR YEARLY PLAN FOR SAVINGS SUCCESS

If one tool has helped me achieve my financial goals over the years, it would be this next worksheet. I truly use all of the sheets you have seen throughout this book and they have all assisted me over the years, but this next one has always helped me break down my goals into monthly and twice-monthly amounts that I know I can make happen. I call this figure the financial independence factor (FI Factor) and without it your financial future is a pipe dream at best. The next worksheet will help you determine your FI Factor and create a detailed annual plan for savings success.

I realize you're attempting to get out of debt and stay out of debt, and now I'm asking you to save, too. Bottom line: you have to save, for a variety of reasons. For one thing, it's important to tell your brain that you aren't working all day long simply to get out and stay out of debt, but that you're also putting something away each month for *you* and your future. Over the years at my seminars and in my one-on-one coaching, some people have commented that my minimum standard of saving 10% along with the other two objectives can be asking too much of them. I struggle with the answer to this, but I would rather see you make significant progress on your debts first, especially if they include revolving charges and consumer debt. I would also suggest that you make your Cookie Jar Factor a priority because it won't do you any good do to pay down your debt only to get back into it again. Then you need to see what you can realistically and consistently commit to each month for your savings plan. If it has to be less than 10% in the beginning, then let it be but do all you can to get as close as possible to 10%. If you receive some type of income increase over the next several months, be sure to reassess this part of your plan ASAP. Also, you may want to go back through the Cut the Fat and Spend Smart exercises in chapter 9 and see where you can make even more changes to save more.

Table 10.8 shows a sample plan. Please review it and take the time right now to create your own plan using the table 10.9. The idea here is to create a detailed plan about not only what or how much you will save, but *where specifically* you will put that money (which account) and how much you will commit to putting away *monthly* to reach your overall goal.

I believe the main reason people don't achieve their savings goals is that the goals are too general and their brains don't know what to focus on to achieve the goal. Your brain is like a computer: you have to give it details of what you specifically want it to do to achieve the desired outcome. Remember that another objective here is to make sure you create a *sustainable amount*—not something that just looks good on paper but something you can really achieve over time.

TABLE 10.8 SAMPLE ONE-YEAR SAVINGS PLAN

My Name: Matt & Kate Bowman   **% of income committed:** 10%

Gross monthly income: $6,000   **Total amount:** $600

Today's date: 1/1/2008

Account Institution / Type of Investment	Goal Total	Current Balance	Amount Left to Save	Monthly Savings
ABC Bank / 401(k)	$2,000	$0	$2,000	$167
ABC Bank / IRA	$2,000	$0	$2,000	$167
Any Bank / Money Market	$1,600	$0	$1,600	$133
Any Brokerage / Portfolio	$1,600	$0	$1,600	$133
Savings Totals:	$7,200	$0	$7,200	$600

These are the savings goals I commit to achieving this year.

TABLE 10.9 MY ONE-YEAR SAVINGS PLAN

My Name:_____   **% of income committed:**____%

Gross monthly income:_$_____   **Total amount:**_$_____

Today's date:_____

Account Institution / Type of Investment	Goal Total	Current Balance	Amount Left to Save	Monthly Savings
	$	$	$	$
	$	$	$	$
	$	$	$	$
	$	$	$	$
	$	$	$	$
	$	$	$	$
Savings Totals:	$	$	$	$

These are the savings goals I commit to achieving this year.

I'm doing my best not to beat a dead horse and I truly hope you get, at this point in the program, how important saving is. Make it an absolute must every single month to put something toward your financial future and independence goals. Don't come up with excuses each month, each quarter, and each year for why you didn't follow through. Set a new standard for yourself and your family that you will save something (ideally a minimum of 10% of your gross) every single month, no matter what. If you can save more, that's fantastic. It will accelerate your independence goals and open your financial world as you prove to the universe that you are "wise with

gold." It is the law of attraction at work for you. Take care of your money and you'll see it take care of you. Ignore it and it will go away.

One action you could take *right now* is to set up an automatic monthly transfer from your checking account to your savings account. If you make it automatic, you won't have to think about it. If you didn't list this in your goal worksheet, automating your savings deposits would be a great pathway goal to add.

Your Financial Tri-Factor

When I started doing one-on-one coaching and calculating people's monthly expenses, I noticed that they typically seemed to be missing three components:

- How much was going toward their debt in addition to their minimum monthly payments (DEA Factor)

- How much was going into some form of planned future expense (Cookie Jar Factor)

- How much was committed each month for true savings (Financial Independence Factor)

These three components are your triple crown for financial success. As we finish this chapter, I'd like you to take a few minutes to write your New Spending Plan for Total Financial Success, including the Tri-Factor components listed above. Simply go to your Cut the Fat exercise (table 9.1) and use the information to fill in the numbers on the following worksheet. Then refer back to your CREDiT plan for your DEA Factor (table 5.3), your Cookie Jar totals (table 8.1), and your FI Factor from your savings plan (lower right corner of table 10.9).

TABLE 10.10 MY NEW SPENDING PLAN FOR TOTAL FINANCIAL SUCCESS

1. Rent or Property Taxes:	$
2. Food—Groceries Only:	$
3. Clothing/Grooming:	$
4. Auto/Transportation:	$
5. Insurances:	$
6. Utilities:	$
7. Minimum Debt Payments:	$
My DEA Factor (from table 5.3)	$
My Cookie Jar Factor (from table 8.1)	$
My Monthly FI Factor (from table 10.9)	$
Business Expenses:	$
Child Expenses:	$
Clubs/Organizations:	$
Contribution:	$
Education:	$
Electronics/Technology:	$
Food—Dining Out:	$

Financial/Banking:	$
Fun/Entertainment:	$
Gifts:	$
Grooming:	$
Habits:	$
Hobbies/Activities:	$
Household Groceries:	$
Household Items:	$
Household Maintenance:	$
Household Staff/Support:	$
Legal/Professional Fees:	$
Luxury Items:	$
Medical/Dental/Alternative:	$
Personal Accessories:	$
Pet Care:	$
Rentals/Properties:	$
Toys:	$
Travel/Vacations:	$
Total of All Monthly Expenses:	$

The next step to making sure everything works in harmony is to look at your total monthly income and subtract your new total monthly expenses to make sure your plan is sustainable. If it is, then you can move on. If it is not, then you may need to go back to the Cut the Fat exercise to see where else you can make some cuts. If at all possible you want to avoid cutting your DEA Factor, Cookie Jar Factor, or FI Factor. Do what it takes right now to make this plan work!

You may have to make some extremely tough decisions about things you may have to do without in order to put this plan into place. There will be a big payoff down the road! You don't want to come this far only to create a plan that doesn't work. Conversely, if you have an overage each month, then my suggestion would be to figure out how you want to divide it within your Tri-Factors to accelerate your critical plan.

TABLE 10.11 PLAN SUMMARY BALANCE CHECK

Total Monthly Income (from Table 2.5):	$
New Total Monthly Expenses (from Table 10.10):	$
Difference (positive or negative):	$

Congratulations! You have just completed the majority of the program for total financial success. Really give yourself some credit here, since most people don't take five minutes to write up a plan, much less all the time, effort, and focus you have put into making this happen.

We now have two final chapters to go. Are you excited? Are you fired up? I am! These next two chapters contain some final ideas, thoughts, and suggestions to get you moving in the new direction for your financial future.

Second only to freedom, learning is the most precious option on earth.

~ Norman Cousins

CHAPTER ELEVEN
Putting It All Together

Let me start this short chapter with a piece of practical expectation. *You will get off course!* Now I'm sure you're wondering why I would say such a thing. Let me offer you an analogy I have found to be most profound.

I recently had a conversation with an airplane pilot who told me that airplanes are off course 80% of the time when they fly. Factors like wind, fuel, air temperature, and even someone getting up to use the restroom constantly knock an airplane off its course. "In fact," the pilot said, "*getting to the destination is nothing but the process of constantly correcting being off course.*" Achieving financial independence works in exactly the same way. In a few short pages, let me give you some quick ideas that will help you stay on course more often than not.

CREATE YOUR OFFICE OR WORK SPACE

When I started this journey back in 1989, I cleared out half of my closet. I kept my clothes on one side, put a small oak desk and my personal development books and files on the other side, and called it my office. You need to have a dedicated place to work. If you're using a computer, you probably already have a den, workplace, or other space where you keep your computer and other materials. It doesn't matter if it's

the kitchen table; you just need a place where you can focus and get things done in a timely fashion to keep your new business on track.

Schedule Your Time

Make time in your schedule each week and each month to stay on top of the tasks at hand. Make it a ritual, just like mowing the lawn or changing the oil in your car. Set a time during the week, such as each Sunday night or every Saturday morning, where you can devote the necessary time to update your information, assess your current status, and set a plan for the week ahead. If you have to, skip that TV show and make this a priority. When you set aside time in advance you will make it happen. Conversely, if you attempt to get to it when you can, it won't happen.

Keep an In-Box

Keeping an in-box is an essential step in getting and staying organized. Brian Tracy, author of many books on management and leadership, has a great criterion for the things you can do with the items in your in-box. He calls it the TRAF system:

T = Trash it

R = Redirect it (give it to someone else)

A = Act on it

F = File it

Organize Your Files

Keeping organized is a key part of your financial business success. Make sure you keep strict accounts by organizing your paperwork just like you would in any other business endeavor. An efficient filing system helps you stay organized, relieves stress, and makes your life much easier and enjoyable. Knowing where things are frees your mind from the struggle of trying to remember where everything is. You file it, it's done, and you can forget about it and live your life.

The following could be a sample of how to chunk or organize your file drawers:

- All portfolio and investment paperwork
- Estate planning and legal files
- All insurance paperwork
- All mortgage and home paperwork
- All credit card and loan paperwork
- Utilities paperwork
- All tax paperwork
- All clubs/subscription paperwork
- Any warranty documents or critical receipts

CLEAN HOUSE

Don't keep things forever! At least once per year, you should purge the paperwork, statements, and receipts you no longer need. Keeping a lean filing system will free your mind to focus on the important tasks rather than on the clutter you have to deal with "someday." Here are a few tips and guidelines for doing so.

- **Bank statements:** Keep monthly statements for one year and keep annual statements for at least seven years. These days, I recommend signing up for electronic statements so you have access to them via computer and the Web.

- **Tax returns and receipts:** Keep tax paperwork for at least seven years, although you may consider keeping them indefinitely. Include canceled checks and receipts for all deductions, W-2 and 1099 forms, mortgage interest statements, and property tax records. Banker's boxes work well for archiving this type of important documentation.

- **Retirement/savings plan and investment statements:** Keep all annual summaries until you retire or close the account.

- **Insurance documents:** Keep your insurance records for five to seven years.

- **IRA contributions:** Keep these records permanently. Keep your records of nondeductible contributions to prove at withdrawal that you already paid tax on this money.

- **House records:** Keep home improvement receipts and records of expenses incurred in selling a home for six years after you sell the home. These expenses can reduce capital gains taxes when you sell the home.

- **Paycheck stubs:** Keep for one year, and keep year-end stubs for seven years. Store these with your tax documents.

- **Bills (phone, utility, etc.):** Keep these records for one year. If you itemize them for tax deductions, keep them for seven years.

- **Personal property:** Keep statements related to large purchases indefinitely, and keep statements related to warranties for the duration of the warranty. Store them in an insurance file for proof of value.

In general you should shred daily records such as ATM and credit card receipts (unless used for tax purposes) after you check them against your monthly statements. Shred monthly and quarterly statements when you receive your annual statements. For filing, I recommend 1.5-inch three-ring binders along with hanging file folders. Schedule time to go through your files once each year to make room for the year ahead.

CREATE A LIBRARY FOR SUCCESS

There is an old saying that if you want to have something, *make it a study*. If you want to have happiness, read books about being happy. If you want to have a great marriage, read books about relationships and making marriage work. Build your library and refer back to your books when you feel like you need a boost or reminder of these fundamentals of success. Hopefully this won't be the only time you read this book to glean the ideas set forth.

INVEST IN TOOLS FOR SUCCESS

One of the best investments you will make is investing in tools for your success. The software programs I mentioned earlier (such as Quicken and Microsoft Money) will eventually be unavoidable for you as you begin to build your wealth and create independence. I've also created some additional tools that you can purchase from my Web site should you choose to do so. I created these tools to help you get to your destination as fast as possible and with as little pain as possible (learning from other people's mistakes rather than from your own).

ACCESS YOUR REPORTS AND REVIEW THEM DAILY, WEEKLY, MONTHLY

As I've suggested throughout this book, please use some type of financial computer program to manage your finances. With this in place you'll be able to run and print various reports. If you carry a planner or notebook, you can put your printed goals inside and keep in constant contact with them. You can also post your goals and reports in places

where you'll see them daily. Remember, out of sight means out of mind. Keep your goals in plain sight, making your targets something you see clearly and often.

LOVE YOUR FAMILY, CHOOSE YOUR PEERS

You're probably wondering, *What do my family and friends have to do with my financial success?* They have a lot to do with what you do or don't accomplish economically. You've probably heard the old saying, "If you lie down with dogs, you come up with fleas." Take a look at who you're spending your valuable time with. Are you spending much of your time with people who are either not committed to a level of financial success or, even worse, who think negatively of people who are?

Now you're probably thinking, "Chris, are you asking me to walk away from my negative friends?" The answer to that question is no, don't walk away from them. *Run* away from your negative friends! In all seriousness, I'm asking you to love your friends and care about them, but please don't let them drag you down if you've made some real decisions, either through this book or through other learning experiences you may have had. Perhaps you can challenge your friends to step up this area of their own lives and make changes or growth of their own. This works in the opposite way as well. If you have family or friends who are doing extremely well, spend more time with them. Call that long-lost rich uncle or aunt and tell them you're coming for the weekend! The truth is, you become like the people you spend your time with.

My wife and I have some very good friends who were always going out for decadent, expensive meals. They were important people in our lives and we wanted to nurture our relationship, but it got to the point where we had to say we would not be joining them at XYZ restaurant but would be happy to join them at a less expensive option. At one point I questioned our friends about how much they were spending on meals each month and whether they were saving anything for their future. They weren't saving much, but as a result of our conversation they put a plan in place to save more than they ever had. We now go to a little pizza joint and eat inexpensive meals together, and every once in a while we go somewhere very nice.

CHOOSE ADVISORS WISELY

Depending on where you are in your journey you'll eventually need professional advice. This list would include:

- Tax attorney or advisor
- Certified Public Accountant (CPA)
- Estate planner/attorney
- Certified Financial Planner (CFP)
- Insurance planner (I typically recommend a CFP to oversee this type of advice)
- Mortgage planner (be careful here)
- A coach (someone to help hold you accountable and offer resources)

The big key here is to find someone who produces *results*, not just someone who sells some type of services you may not need.

AUTOMATE WHEREVER POSSIBLE

We live in a world filled with technology and conveniences that can help us accomplish our goals and dreams much easier than in previous times. An additional benefit to these advances is the ability to leverage the discipline necessary to achieve these goals. When I speak of automation,

I'm speaking of services offered by banking and financial institutions such as direct deposits and electronic funds transfers (EFT). If you haven't done so already, make it a goal to automate many of your financial transactions, such as bill paying and transfers between accounts.

Two of the most important tools you could set up right now would be to automate your number one target from your Debt Elimination Plan (the minimum monthly payment plus your DEA Factor) and your mortgage payment, if you have one. You can also automate many of your consistent monthly payments such as your auto, phone, electric, and cable bills.

If you have a 401(k) at work and aren't contributing to it, contact your plan administrator (possibly someone in your Human Resources department) to set one up. If you're somewhat undisciplined you might use a program like Bank of America's "Keep the Change" plan where they round up your debit card transactions to the nearest dollar and deposit the difference into your savings account. I realize there are upsides and downsides to a program like this but if you truly save the money (meaning you don't inevitably withdraw and spend it) there can be an ultimate advantage. You can also set up automatic transfers from your checking or savings account into another account (money market, brokerage account), and you can do this for your Cookie Jar Factor as well. This is something I do and highly recommend.

Two Additional Tools to Use

A fantastic tool I've used for years to help me keep my financial commitments is a sheet I call my Monthly Savings and Expense Deposits (also known as Buckets and Jars). I've provided a sample for you (table 10.12) and a blank worksheet (table 10.13) so you can summarize your monthly commitments. You can either put a checkmark in the monthly boxes when each one is completed or you can write in the actual amount of the deposit so you can track in detail.

TABLE 10.12 SAMPLE MONTHLY SAVINGS AND EXPENSE DEPOSITS

Account	Monthly Goal	Jan	Feb	Mar	April	May	June	July	Aug	Sept	Oct	Nov	Dec	On Track?
Buckets														
My Savings and Investment Buckets														
ABC Bank	$167	$167	$167	$167	$	$	$	$	$	$	$	$	$	Yes
ABC Bank	$167	$167	$167	$167	$	$	$	$	$	$	$	$	$	Yes
Any Bank	$133	$133	$133	$133	$	$	$	$	$	$	$	$	$	Yes
Brokerage	$133	$133	$133	$133	$	$	$	$	$	$	$	$	$	Yes
Mo Total:	$600	$600	$600	$600	$	$	$	$	$	$	$	$	$	
Jars														
My Cookie Jar Spending Plan														
Vacation	$134	$134	$134	$134	$	$	$	$	$	$	$	$	$	Yes
Car Repair	$125	$125	$125	$125	$	$	$	$	$	$	$	$	$	Yes
Patio Furn.	$100	$100	$100	$100	$	$	$	$	$	$	$	$	$	Yes
Education	$113	$113	$113	$113	$	$	$	$	$	$	$	$	$	Yes
Clothing	$100	$100	$100	$50	$	$	$	$	$	$	$	$	$	No
Mo Total:	$572	$572	$572	$522	$	$	$	$	$	$	$	$	$	

TABLE 10.13 MY MONTHLY SAVINGS AND EXPENSE DEPOSITS

Account	Monthly Goal	Jan	Feb	Mar	April	May	June	July	Aug	Sept	Oct	Nov	Dec	On Track?
Buckets						My Savings and Investment Buckets								
	$	$	$	$	$	$	$	$	$	$	$	$	$	
	$	$	$	$	$	$	$	$	$	$	$	$	$	
	$	$	$	$	$	$	$	$	$	$	$	$	$	
	$	$	$	$	$	$	$	$	$	$	$	$	$	
	$	$	$	$	$	$	$	$	$	$	$	$	$	
	$	$	$	$	$	$	$	$	$	$	$	$	$	
Mo Total:	$	$	$	$	$	$	$	$	$	$	$	$	$	
Jars						My Cookie Jar Spending Plan								
	$	$	$	$	$	$	$	$	$	$	$	$	$	
	$	$	$	$	$	$	$	$	$	$	$	$	$	
	$	$	$	$	$	$	$	$	$	$	$	$	$	
	$	$	$	$	$	$	$	$	$	$	$	$	$	
	$	$	$	$	$	$	$	$	$	$	$	$	$	
	$	$	$	$	$	$	$	$	$	$	$	$	$	
Mo Total:	$	$	$	$	$	$	$	$	$	$	$	$	$	

Last, I have a fun sheet that my clients have used over the years to track both cash and electronic expenses (debit/credit). I call it My Daily/Weekly Cash Expense Totals. I don't use this sheet anymore, but I did when getting started with this material. The objective of this sheet is to track all of your little expenses (especially cash) and come up with two totals for evaluation. The first is a total of how much you spend daily, and the second is how much you spend over the course of a week on a particular expense (like breakfast or snacks). These little expenses can add up to a significant amount over a period of 10 or 20 years, so you want to get a handle on them now. Electronic versions of both of these sheets are available on my Website at www.5MinuteDebtSolution.com.

THE **5minute** DEBT SOLUTION

TABLE 10.14 DAILY/WEEKLY CASH EXPENSE TOTALS

Type	Monday	Tuesday	Wed	Thursday	Friday	Saturday	Sunday	Week Total
Breakfast	$	$	$	$	$	$	$	$
Lunch	$	$	$	$	$	$	$	$
Snacks	$	$	$	$	$	$	$	$
Dinner	$	$	$	$	$	$	$	$
Gifts	$	$	$	$	$	$	$	$
Contributions	$	$	$	$	$	$	$	$
Fuel	$	$	$	$	$	$	$	$
Coffee/Soda	$	$	$	$	$	$	$	$
	$	$	$	$	$	$	$	$
	$	$	$	$	$	$	$	$
Daily Total	$	$	$	$	$	$	$	$

"You can't measure what you don't monitor."
~ Anthony Robbins

To know even one life has breathed easier because you have lived. This is to have succeeded.

~ Ralph Waldo Emerson

CHAPTER TWELVE

Beyond Financial Freedom: The True Purpose of Wealth

In 1989 when I was 26 years old, I had $25,000 in debts, no savings, and a future that was not looking too bright. Although I thought I was fairly happy, I certainly wasn't living up to my capabilities and I really didn't have a plan for my life, let alone my finances. Then something happened and my life would never be the same: I met my good friend Tony Robbins.

I've learned a great deal from Tony over nearly two decades but the single most important lesson I learned is this: *The secret to living is giving.* I have to admit that when I first heard this, the idea did not seem relevant or seize me in the moment. Because I was so far in the hole financially, I couldn't even entertain the thought of benevolence. Later that year I was invited to Thanksgiving dinner at Tony's Del Mar castle (yes, it's actually a landmark building in northern San Diego built as a Spanish colonial castle). I remember thinking to myself, *Cool, a free dinner!* But there was a caveat: the invitation included a request to bring two baskets of food for two needy families. I must confess that a free dinner at Dad's house sounded much easier and less painful at the time, but for some reason I was pulled in the direction of an RSVP and I promised to show up with the baskets.

I remember standing in line at the grocery store as if it were yesterday. I had pennies in my pocket, I had nothing in the bank, my

credit cards were maxed out, and I was holding one in my hand to pay for this shopping spree. I had never filled a basket of groceries like this before, not even for myself, and I had no idea how I was going to pay for all the food. As I left the store on that cool November afternoon, even though I was financially at rock bottom, somehow *I felt wealthier in that moment than I had ever felt in my entire life.* Truthfully, I needed someone to bring *me* a basket of food, but for the first time ever, I was putting the needs of someone else above my own—someone I didn't even know! Until that day, my idea of Thanksgiving had been stuffing my own face, drinking beer, and screaming at anyone who blocked my view of the TV during the big games.

Later that day, about 60 of us went to a community center near the Mexican border to deliver the baskets face-to-face. It was truly a day I will never forget. As I watched people receive their gifts, a woman and her young daughter handed me a note, which I have to this day. It read:

> *Thank you very much for this food.*
> *If it wasn't for this gift from you, my family*
> *would not have had a Thanksgiving dinner.*

I started crying. The woman hugged me, and her little girl hugged me. To realize that I had played a part in creating this magic moment was absolutely incredible and addictive. Although I am now extremely motivated to do well for myself and my family, I can honestly tell you that no amount of money could ever buy the level of gratitude and abundance I felt that day. I learned that the secret to feeling wealthy is to *take the time right now to think about all that you are grateful for and focus on all the abundance you have in your life.* When you do that, fear and scarcity melt away and you'll be the wealthiest person on earth.

CREATING AN ATTITUDE OF ABUNDANCE

Let me ask you a question: Do you live your life by the belief that there isn't enough to go around or do you feel that the world is abundant and there's plenty for everyone? There's a big difference between being deliberate and focused with your money and coming from a place of lack or scarcity. When you associate money with scarcity, you're coming from a place of *fear*.

What does an attitude of abundance mean and how can you create one within yourself? Understanding this issue requires a different and unique perspective. Someone can have millions of dollars in the bank but come from a place of scarcity and fear, while someone who hasn't a penny in the bank can come from a place of total abundance and freedom. The real issue here is *wealth,* not money. To have true wealth, you must be grateful for what you have and believe that there will always be enough for you. As you play the financial game, try to understand where you're coming from so you can make any necessary adjustments. I often remember that Thanksgiving in 1989 when I had less money than I'd ever had, was literally at my financial bottom, yet I felt wealthier than I ever had in my entire lifetime. The difference for me was that I stepped outside myself to help someone who had far less than me, and it felt amazing.

Today, the Anthony Robbins Foundation feeds over four million people a year in over 80 countries—and I'm proud to say that my wife and I have contributed to this Basket Brigade every year since that first year in 1989. It's always a great reminder of where we have come from and it makes us very grateful for our own journey.

JUST LIKE MY CHILD FOUNDATION

Recently a close friend of mine, Vivian Glyck, felt a strong call to witness for herself the situation of the millions of children orphaned by AIDS in Africa. Following her own internal voice, Vivian took her

first trip to Africa with a group affiliated with the Agape Spiritual Center in Los Angeles. When she returned from her trip, she solidified her new mission in life and started the Just Like My Child Foundation (www.justlikemychild.org).

The Just Like My Child Foundation is focused on assisting mothers and children in rural Uganda, East Africa by tackling the root causes of poverty through education, health care, and micro-enterprise. Vivian's goal is to have a direct impact on a community of 48 villages and over 600,000 people through the work of Just Like My Child.

Why Africa? I know there are many children in this country who need love and care. I know there are children living in poverty and despair with no hope to carry them through the day. But when I hear statistics like the following, my heart turns to Africa, too. According to the 2007 AIDS Epidemic Update prepared by the Joint United Nations Program on HIV/AIDS (UNAIDS) and the World Health Organization:

- In 2007, HIV/AIDS killed 1.6 million people in sub-Saharan Africa (an average of 4,400 per day).

- Approximately 1.7 million people in sub-Saharan Africa were newly infected with HIV that year (4,700 per day), bringing the region's total to 22.5 million.

- Roughly 11.4 million children have lost one or both parents to AIDS.

- More than two out of three (68%) adults and nearly 90% of children infected with HIV live in sub-Saharan Africa, and more than three in four (76%) AIDS deaths in 2007 occurred there.

These children are just like our own children. They're funny, smart, and full of love. As actor Brad Pitt said, "You want to gather up handfuls of them and bring them home." This is why Vivian named her nonprofit foundation the Just Like My Child Foundation, Inc. and why my family and I are so very proud to donate 10% of our proceeds of this book to her foundation and mission. One of the reasons I selected my partner in publishing this book is because they will make their own contribution as well with each book sold.

It's not my intent to tell you what or who to support. However, I urge you to find something you believe in and give unconditionally. Contribution not only answers the highest calling of our souls, it also has a miraculous effect of bringing more to you, not only spiritually, but often financially. The very word for money, *currency*, means "a flow"—there's a life force to it. What you allow to flow out will flow back.

Make contribution a part of your spending plan, whether you do it monthly, quarterly, or yearly. Just like every other expense, plan it in accordance with your other goals and objectives.

PUTTING THIS BOOK INTO PERSPECTIVE

For the most part, this entire book has been about money and personal finances. I truly hope I haven't given you the impression that money should be the most important thing to focus on in life. I certainly wouldn't want that. My intent with this book was to provide a tool for those who lack a practical education in this area and for those who simply have not focused on this part of life and have decided that now is the time to make it more important.

I think it's fair to say that we can focus on only a few major areas of our lives. They include health, relationships, emotional well-being, finances, spirituality or religion, time management, and career. It's not my place to tell you which area should be most important, because it's all a balancing act, isn't it? There are times or stages when family may be most important to you, and times when career may top your list. We all

need to keep health up there at the top or we could have real trouble. If this is a time for you to make your financial life more important, then by all means I want you to do so, but not at the expense of other areas. I personally use a system that allows me to make sure I check in with every area frequently. If you don't have a system to manage your time and your life I would certainly make a hard argument that you find one. There's a big difference between saying, "I need to go to the bank and open an IRA" and "I will go to the bank this Friday at 9:30 AM and take 20 minutes to open an IRA for my future savings deposits." The second statement has much more power because it is specific, measurable, and has a time frame attached. These three elements make you more likely to follow through— especially if you have some real, compelling reasons behind them.

As you read the final words of this labor of love, please make sure you create some type of system to check in on what you have created here. Block out a day of the week and a time of the day to make progress on your goals. I promise, the more you check in and follow up, the more likely you will be to make progress.

OUR DECLARATION OF INDEPENDENCE

Have you ever wondered what happened to the 56 men who signed the Declaration of Independence? I'd like to offer you a brief history lesson about the ultimate destinies of these men and their families. This information appears on a variety of Internet sites. Several of them credit Rush Limbaugh as the source; others cite Mary Needham, president of the Reserve Technological Institute; and at least one attributes it to Gary Hildreth of Erie, Pennsylvania. I'm not sure who to acknowledge for this powerfully moving essay but I gratefully include it with the hope that you will follow and pursue your noble goal of creating personal financial independence.

"The Price They Paid"

Five of the signers were captured by the British as traitors and tortured before they died. Twelve had their homes ransacked and burned. Two lost their sons serving in the Revolutionary Army, and another had two sons captured. Nine of the fifty-six fought and died from wounds or hardships of the Revolutionary War. These men signed and pledged their lives, their fortunes, and their sacred honor. What kind of men were they? Twenty-four were lawyers and jurists. Eleven were merchants; nine were farmers and large plantation owners, men of means, well educated. But they signed the Declaration of Independence knowing full well that the penalty would be death if they were captured.

Carter Braxton of Virginia, a wealthy planter and trader, saw his ships swept from the seas by the British navy. He sold his home and properties to pay his debts and died in rags. Thomas McKeam was so hounded by the British that he was forced to move his family almost constantly, his possessions were taken from him, and poverty was his reward. Vandals or soldiers looted the properties of Dillery, Hall, Clymer, Walton, Gwinnett, Heyward, Ruttledge, and Middleton. It continues.

At the battle of Yorktown, Thomas Nelson, Jr. noted that the British General Cornwallis had taken over the Nelson home for his headquarters. He quietly urged General George Washington to open fire. The home was destroyed, and Nelson died bankrupt. Francis Lewis had his home and properties destroyed. The enemy jailed his wife, and she died within a few months. John Hart was driven from his wife's bedside as she was dying.

Such were the stories and sacrifices of the American Revolution. These were not crazy, wild-eyed ruffians. They were soft-

spoken men of means and education. They had security, but they valued liberty more. Standing tall, straight, and unwavering, they pledged: "For the support of this declaration, with firm reliance on the protection of the divine providence, we mutually pledge to each other our lives, our fortunes, and our sacred honor."

They gave you and me a free and *independent* America. The history books never told us a lot of what happened in the Revolutionary War. The colonials didn't just fight the British, they were British subjects at that time and they fought their own government. After the war, most of the surviving delegates served their new government. Two signers became U.S. presidents (Adams and Jefferson). Two had sons who became president (Adams and Harrison).

Unfortunately some of us take these liberties for granted. We shouldn't. Please take a minute or two as you finish this book and ask yourself, knowing that you have the liberty, Do I owe it to myself, my family, and the spirit of these great people to achieve my own financial independence? Fifty-six men signed the Declaration of Independence, all fully aware that the punishment for treason was death by hanging or dismemberment. They did this for me and they did this for you.

It's Been a True Honor

If you've gotten this far and you've used what was presented and taught in these pages, I sincerely applaud you. Even if you simply scanned through this book and it caused you to rethink some things or gain a new perspective, I applaud you as well. At this point, I trust that you know this book was written purely from my heart to teach, inspire, and motivate. Writing these pages has been a dream for many years and closing them out is a bittersweet experience. It's bittersweet to me that this project has come to an end for now, and terrifically exciting knowing that it may help even one person to improve his or her financial situation. Maybe that person will be you. Whatever you decide for yourself, I wish you only the best in your financial journey. If I can serve you in any way, I invite you to contact me directly through my Web site at www.5MinuteDebtSolution.com, if only to let me know how this book has impacted you or to send any comments or stories you'd like to share about your journey and experience.

A FINAL REQUEST FOR YOUR CONSIDERATION

In 1999, I was going through a pretty rough period in my marriage, and my wife and I temporarily separated. A very good friend of mine had read a book on relationships that he encouraged me to buy and read. Out of desperation I did just that. David Deida titled the book *The Way of the Superior Man*, and I can honestly say *that book saved my marriage.* It was exactly what I needed at the time and without it we would surely have divorced.

You never know how powerfully a book can impact your life or the life of someone you know. I ask that you consider letting the people you know and care about—people who could use the words on these pages to improve their own circumstances—that this material is available to them. You never know what will come back to you as a result of your recommendation. Do you think I ever let my friend forget that he played a role in improving the quality of my life? Hardly! And when I do remind him, he gets the joy of knowing that he has made a difference in the lives of a family, as my wife and I have had two children as a result of getting back together.

Use what you learned, share what you learned, and I hope that someday our paths will cross and we'll get to meet personally. Until that day, I wish you all the best in your quest for a great quality of life and future financial independence.

Glossary of Terms and Intellectual Property Of Eighty/Twenty Technologies, Inc.

Take Count®

The process of counting all of your financial assets, liabilities, income, and expenses and then evaluating your current financial condition using the Money Metrics™ system.

Money Metrics™

A series of measuring points to determine the overall health of your financial position compared to what you would like to achieve economically.

The CREDiT Method™

A five-step process for creating a compelling plan to get out of debt forever. The acronym stands for Capture, Resolve, Execute, Decide and invest, Terminate.

Cookie Jar Factor™

A strategy and tool for staying out of debt. The process includes the strategy of planning for major expenses *in advance*, in order to pay cash for them and eliminate the need for borrowing.

Destined for Wealth™

The title of my six-session, one-on-one coaching system and one-day intensive seminar, which includes all the content from this book in a workshop environment.

About The Author

For nearly two decades, Chris Hendrickson has inspired people to get out and stay out of debt. During this time he has also been a trainer, teacher, and top sales producer with the Anthony Robbins Companies.

Chris began his career in personal finance and consumer credit in 1986. Working with Household Finance Corporation, he served as a loan officer, debt collector, bankruptcy representative, and repossession official. Seeing the negative impact a lack of education and poor financial habits made on people's lives, Chris developed a mission to educate and inspire people to improve their personal finances.

In 1989, Chris teamed up with Tony Robbins—a world leader in self-improvement and personal coaching—to empower thousands of people to finally get out of debt and stay out of debt forever. Chris is certified in Human Needs Psychology as a peak performance expert and has worked as a consultant in the financial, real estate, sales, and telemarketing industries. He developed *The 5-Minute Debt Solution* to help busy people define a plan to end the burden of debt and achieve their personal financial dreams.

Chris studied directly under many of the world's top financial experts, including Tony Robbins; investors John Templeton and Peter Lynch; and economic forecasters Paul Zane Pilzer, Harry Dent, and Robert Prechter. Chris has also been a featured speaker at Robbins's Wealth Mastery seminars, a four-day live program taught in seven countries around the world. He also collaborated on the creation of Robbins's Financial Freedom coaching program.

A San Diego resident since 1973, Chris lives with his wife and two sons in Del Mar, California. He is available for speaking engagements and one-on-one coaching. For more information, contact:

info@5minutedebtsolution.com

A free special offer to the purchasers of this book
FREE "DEBT TO WEALTH" Video Bonus

Learn how Chris went from being $25,000 in credit card debt, not a penny in the bank to a multi-millionaire. Chris will show you how you can go from broke to wealthy for yourself and your family in this easy-to-follow, dynamic presentation.

In less than 50 minutes, Chris will teach you:

- The 8 areas of financial focus (and where you need to focus your attention now)
- The Cycle of Money for maximum returns
- 3 Ways to save more
- The #1 killer of your financial success
- Getting to YOUR number for financial independence
- The one thing you can do RIGHT NOW to start!

Download this free video at: www.TakeCount.com

If you prefer, you can get it on DVD, free (just $7 for shipping and handling).

Mail to: ETTI, 13024 Sandown Way, Suite 100, San Diego, CA 92130-3739

CPSIA information can be obtained at www.ICGtesting.com
Printed in the USA
BVOW040314280212

283985BV00004B/6/P